A COACH IN PROGRESS

A COACH IN PROGRESS

MARSHALL FOOTBALL—A STORY OF SURVIVAL AND REVIVAL

BY RED DAWSON
WITH PATRICK GARBIN

FOREWORDS BY BOBBY BOWDEN AND FRED BILETNIKOFF

SPORTS PUBLISHING

Sports Publishing books may be purchased in bulk at special discounts for sales promotion, corporate gifts, fund-raising, or educational purposes. Special editions can also be created to specifications. For details, contact the Special Sales Department, Sports Publishing, 307 West 36th Street, 11th Floor, New York, NY 10018 or sportspubbooks@skyhorsepublishing.com.

Sports Publishing® is a registered trademark of Skyhorse Publishing, Inc.®, a Delaware corporation.

Visit our website at www.sportspubbooks.com.

10 9 8 7 6 5 4 3 2

Library of Congress Cataloging-in-Publication Data is available on file.

Cover design by Tom Lau
Cover photo: Dr. Joseph Chambers

ISBN: 978-1-61321-822-8
Ebook ISBN 978-1-61321-849-5
Printed in the United States of America

CONTENTS

To the seventy-five people of Marshall who lost their lives on November 14, 1970, but whose spirits will live for eternity.
—R.D.

To Elizabeth, Trip, and Rebecca, who give me their constant love and encouragement.
To my late Herschel—a DGD!
To the seventy-five we will never forget, who gave their lives for a fine university and its accomplished football program.
—P.G.

ACKNOWLEDGMENTS

THERE ARE SO MANY people from my past and present I should recognize for their unconditional support, guidance, and inspiration for this, my first book project, along with many other life experiences, most prominently:

—My father—five-foot-seven, 150-pound Big Jack—for teaching me how to work hard, and encouraging me to be somebody.

—My mother, Big Lou, for being an extraordinary woman, feeding me, and patching my wounds.

—Lewis and Mart Hill, for being great friends, guiding me all my life. And I'll never forget the great hunting.

—All my coaches from junior high through the pros; there's too many to name, although Bobby Bowden was my favorite of favorites.

—Frank Bird, an older friend, who helped rebuild my confidence, which included improving my ability to fish.

—Buddy Coleman and Frank King, friends for life after growing up together in Valdosta, Georgia.

—Lucille Sineath, Rhett Dawson, and the late Jack Dawson, the best siblings anyone could ever have.

—Marshall Hall of Fame golf coach Joe Feaganes, who taught me how to play golf, but I'm still not worth a hoot.

—Marshall University, which saved me from a life of bitterness, especially these individuals: Steve Kopp, Bobby Pruett, Jim Donnan, Doc Holliday, and Bob Marcum. To Bob, you're a tremendously tough man, whom I greatly admire.

—My life love, who also grew up with me in Valdosta, Rosie Alexander, for encouraging me to walk the straight line.

—My children, Katie and Bill Dawson.

—R.D.

For this inspiring and gratifying, yet at times challenging book project on Red Dawson and his affiliation with Marshall University and its football program, there are a number of individuals I need to identify for the support they have given me.

To my three ultimate supporters, to whom this book is partly dedicated; plus, my parents, who have always encouraged me, and still provide even today a proofreading prowess exceeded by few professional editors.

Notably, this is only the second of nine traditionally published books I have authored not focusing on University of Georgia football, and my first that is a single continuous narrative. I would like to acknowledge Skyhorse Publishing for taking a chance on an author encountering subject matter and a writing style I was fairly unaccustomed to, and particularly our editor on the project, Julie Ganz, for her tremendous guidance and extraordinary patience throughout the entire process.

I extend my appreciation to the number of sources who supplied photographs for this book, particularly Debbie Chambers, whose contributions included the cover image taken by her father. Dr. Joseph Chambers was not only an esteemed physician in Huntington but a devoted Marshall supporter who could often be found along the sidelines at Thundering Herd games as the football program's unofficial team photographer. Dr. Chambers and his wife, Peggy, were among the seventy-five who died in the plane crash, leaving Debbie and her sister, Cindy, both Marshall cheerleaders at the time, orphaned. Still, Debbie epitomized the Marshall spirit by continuing to exhibit her unwavering support for the university and its athletic teams.

Last but certainly not least, I want to acknowledge Marshall University, its football program, the people of Huntington, and especially Red Dawson for sharing the moving Marshall spirit with me for a few days in mid-November 2014—a spirit that inspired the writing of this book, and one I have embraced ever since.

—P.G.

FOREWORD
BY BOBBY BOWDEN

WILLIAM (BILL) "RED" DAWSON is as good an example of a "good ole southern country boy" as any I know. Born and raised in Valdosta, Georgia, which is about forty miles north of the southeast Florida line, he attended and starred in football at Valdosta High School. The Wildcats seemed like they won the Georgia State Championship nearly every year under the guidance of Coach Wright Bazemore. Red received a football scholarship to Florida State University and enrolled in 1960. Florida State had been an all-girls school up to 1947, the first official year in which it also fielded a football team.

I came to Tallahassee in January of 1963 as the tight end–receivers coach. I was Dawson's position coach his junior and senior years. He was always one of my favorite players during my fifty-seven years of coaching. He was a "yes, sir" and "no, sir" type of guy who would play his heart out to get the job done. I spent many a practice with Red driving a blocking sled which he pushed all over the field. In 1964, Red's senior year, FSU had its most successful year up to that point climaxed by a Gator Bowl win over Oklahoma, which helped to put Florida State on the map. From FSU, Red went right into pro ball and afterwards into coaching.

Eventually, I went to West Virginia University and became head football coach in 1970. A couple of years before, Red became an assistant coach at Marshall University. There, our paths crossed again. When the Marshall plane crashed in 1970, killing everyone aboard, my initial thought was to wonder if Dawson was on that plane. Watching TV as they released the names of all who died, I kept looking for Red's name. I hoped and prayed he was alive, although I lost other friends in the crash. It was a sad day for me, as well as the whole state of West Virginia.

Due to my relationship with Coach Dawson, I was contacted by Marshall's new head coach, Jack Lengyel, about me helping them with their new offensive plans in the spring of 1971. They had only freshmen available and I invited them to come to my office. For a few days, I allowed them to study our film, peruse our playbook, and get whatever they needed.

Now, let Red tell you the rest of the story. Can you imagine what he had stored up inside him and has hardly ever revealed publicly? I couldn't wait to read his book about the memories and the pain he has carried all these years. I love Red Dawson!

FOREWORD
BY FRED BILETNIKOFF

In 1961, I left my home state of Pennsylvania to attend college and play football at Florida State. Of the thirty to thirty-five newcomers in my class, I was one of only two or three non-southerners, and the only person on the entire team from Pennsylvania. Having to adapt to living in the Deep South was a *real* change for me, so it was rather ironic that the first Seminole player I really got to know, and admire, personified the South—Red Dawson.

Playing with Red on Florida State's varsity team for a few years, including a season when we were team captains, I became very familiar with a teammate who had an extreme passion for football. Red was a tough guy, a hard worker, had a positive attitude all the time, and was often the teammate who led the rest of us. Still, as much as he was appreciated on the field, he might have been even more admired for what he did off the field.

Like most people Red encounters, I found him to have an attractive personality. He was always smiling, very jovial, and made others feel comfortable around him—at ease. Red personified the kind of individual I liked and wanted to associate with. Not long after I arrived at Florida State,

I essentially dismissed the fact I was more than 1,000 miles away from home in a completely different part of the country, but felt very comfortable in Tallahassee—and, mostly because of Red.

It pains me to think that anyone would have to endure the horrific experiences—primarily, the plane crash—Red experienced while coaching at Marshall. But, when someone who seemingly everyone loves and highly respects encounters such tragedy, the heartache is even more agonizing.

In 1970, upon learning of the disaster that occurred to the Marshall football program, I was saddened but, because of my feelings for Red, I was instantly relieved my old teammate and friend wasn't on the plane. However, I soon realized the anguish he must have experienced: how could he bear the hardship of thinking, on one hand, how fortunate he was to not be on the plane yet, because he was so involved with the team, how *un*fortunate he was to be left alive and not among those who perished?

Knowing Red for more than fifty years, the one thing I can say is if you could have only one friend, Red Dawson is the friend you'd want to have. As indicated, he cares for his friends and is concerned about the friendships he cultivated. But, perhaps most importantly, Red has always been the friend who initiates connecting with everyone else. There's no telling how many people were asked—let's say—just today Red's familiar "How you doing?" or "How are things going?" or "How's your family?" He's the ultimate at keeping friendships going—keeping relationships *alive*.

I'm aware of how Red courageously stayed involved with Marshall immediately following the disaster despite facing many roadblocks. But there comes a time when a man—and, believe me, Red was and is a "man" if there ever was one—can only withstand so much.

After many years of a lack of involvement between Red and Marshall, it was a heartwarming moment for me when I heard my friend and the university he once loved so much had reunited. Their relationship was then further heightened with Red's involvement in *We Are Marshall*. The movie allowed Red to heal to some degree, giving him the fortitude to finally discuss some of his old wounds. Still, with every tremendous tragedy, a deep scar remains in some that will never, ever heal. This book should only help in Red's continuing the healing process—if only in the slightest.

Moreover, this book conveys that although a close relationship may falter at some point, it ultimately can become active again. And, I wouldn't expect anything less from Red than keeping yet another relationship *alive*.

INTRODUCTION

NOVEMBER 14, 2014, IS a day I'll never forget—ever. That afternoon, I had one of the most moving experiences of my life when I attended the 44th Annual Marshall University Memorial Service, or the Fountain Ceremony. The service honored the seventy-five individuals who died in a hillside plane crash near Huntington, West Virginia, on November 14, 1970. Nearly all of those who perished were Thundering Herd football players, coaches, and team supporters.

With hundreds in attendance at the memorial, I was fortunate to be there as a guest of William "Bill" Dawson, better known as Red. Although Red and I had known one another for only several months, we had grown relatively close as I had heard intricate details of his life, including specifics about his integral role in building the Marshall football program prior to and after the plane crash, and what he has endured because of the tragedy.

By the time I got to the memorial, my knowledge of Red Dawson was a far cry from what it had been, say, six months prior when, like many people, I was familiar with him only from all the publicity that had surrounded *We Are Marshall*, and from watching the movie itself. It turns out, I was hardly familiar with him at all. However, we would first become acquainted by the most random of circumstances, perhaps transpiring because, borrowing a moniker from Red, the "Old Master" often works in mysterious ways. Simply based on a conversation I had with Red's best friend's son (who I really didn't know that well at the time either), a meeting between the two of us was arranged in Athens, Georgia, where Red's lifelong friend, Rosie, lived—450 miles from Red's home in Huntington—to discuss the possibility of a book project.

Before meeting Red, I conducted extensive research, discovering the man best known as "the Marshall coach not in the plane crash" had experienced quite an event-filled life beyond the tragedy. Around the age of ten, Red was written up in a local newspaper in south Georgia after encountering a red and yellow snake. After reciting to himself the mnemonic, "Red and yellow, kill a fellow; red and black, friend of Jack," Red killed what would eventually be identified as a type of snake that reportedly had not been seen in the area for years, an extremely venomous coral snake. Later as a football player, Red was lauded by legendary Bobby Bowden—the coach's "favorite of favorites"—and, according to Bill Peterson, Red's head coach while at Florida State, he was "one of the best team leaders I have ever been associated with. When Red spoke, his teammates listened."

In recent years, Red made the local news after developing a friendship with a girl from California, who decided to attend Marshall out of high school primarily because of the impression *We Are Marshall* had made on her.

"Uncle Red," as she referred to him, took the girl under his wing during her freshman year, helping her move into her dorm, often checking up on her, and routinely talking her through homesickness.

Never asking for a speaking fee, Red has presented so many speeches since the movie, he could have made another career out of it. From high school teams to doctors to the Daughters of the American Revolution—you name the group—there's a good chance they have asked Red to speak. Each group usually anticipates he will talk about the movie and the survivor's guilt that has hindered him since the plane crash, and Red does. But, no speech of his is complete without his thoughts on leadership, pre-judgment, how to be successful in life, or his mention of "Red's Rules," which include "Never let anybody outwork you at what you do," and "Cultivate the friendship of old men."

Like every non-fiction book project in which I have been involved, I had planned to be up front with Red, firmly establishing that above all, if we were going to work together, we needed to be truthful with one another and truthful with every single word we put to paper. I had come to realize certain extraordinary accounts have been embellished over time to seem even more remarkable. Considering the Marshall tragedy for example, the Young Thundering Herd's miraculous and historical victory over Xavier in 1971 resulted from Marshall entering the game as supposedly 20- or 21-point underdogs (indication of how big of an underdog Marshall was has been claimed numerous times, although never by Red). However, I knew that back in 1971, rarely would "official" odds be set on a caliber game pitting two lower-level independent teams like Marshall and Xavier. Upon further research, the two reputable sources at the time that forecasted the game, the Dunkel Index and the Harmon Forecast, actually projected the contest as an even matchup, and Marshall by three points, respectively.

I also wanted to ask Red about his relationship with Jack Lengyel, Marshall's head coach for four seasons beginning with the 1971 season after the tragedy, and Joe McMullen, Marshall's athletic director hired just before Lengyel. According to an article in a 1980 issue of *Inside Sports*, "Marshall University: How Long Can A Nightmare Last?", the three head coaches McMullen hired during his tenure (Lengyel, Frank Ellwood, and Sonny Randle) all had difficulty working for—"and always for, never with"—the athletic director, who was fired in 1979 and died in 1983 from leukemia. Evidently, McMullen meddled, lacked tact, and the latter two head coaches went so far as insinuating he was a reason why Marshall football struggled mightily during the 1970s. It was clear Red had been instrumental in rebuilding the program following the crash as "acting" head coach; however, it appeared he hadn't even been a candidate to resume the role as soon as McMullen was hired. Also, it seemed Red had conflicts with Lengyel, which had even been indicated as much in an interview with Matthew Fox, the actor who played Red in the movie.

Moreover, in interviews I came across, Red claimed his final season coaching at Marshall was 1971. Yet, I discovered an article of him commenting as a defensive assistant on how impressive Northern Illinois' running game was prior to the Herd's game against the Huskies in 1972.

In researching Red before we finally met, I was also aware that although he was in his early seventies, I probably needed to tread lightly before I "demanded" the truth, or immediately began tossing difficult questions his way. At six-foot-three, 240 pounds, Red was said to still have the same stature as when he played professional football, and the same tough-as-nails persona. According to Matthew Fox in another interview, Red was "like John Wayne." He was supposedly "old man strong"—what I've always known it as—or an older man possessing an uncanny hardening process or toughness, providing him with physical strength and a fighting prowess greater than most men decades younger.

Upon meeting Red, he appeared much as I envisioned him: a big, hardened good ole boy, like a tough cowboy-like figure from an old Western film, and, yes, he indeed seemed "old man strong." After introductions, much to my satisfaction, Red declared that if we were going to do a book together, there had to be "no b.s.—no embellishments." Although *We Are Marshall* was a quality film that did considerable good for a lot of people, especially for him, it contained some "Hollywood fluff," as Red called it. He wanted to tell the absolute truth. He then added that Jesus had seven sins "that He really disliked, and four or five of those were sins of the tongue—gossip, or bearing false witness against your neighbor." Red said like Jesus, he didn't like gossip and, above all, he wanted the truth to be told.

Months later in November, as I drove to Huntington to visit with Red for a few days to resume our project, I was anxious to be exposed to a football program with such continuing progress and success. Marshall was opening its Sports Hall of Fame that weekend, housed in its state-of-the-art indoor practice facility that was unveiled earlier in the football season. Near the facility, an extravagant sculpture of three buffaloes, "Ashes to Glory," by internationally renowned artist Stan Mullins, was planned to be revealed sometime in 2015. On the field, directed by head coach Doc Holliday, the Thundering Herd was undefeated at 9-0, ranked 21st in the nation, and had visions of playing in a major bowl entering that Saturday's home game against Rice.

Marshall football was undoubtedly a far cry from when it had been Red's responsibility to direct the Herd's rebirth from the ruins of an unimaginable tragedy. To start the rebuilding process of a college football program immediately following such tragedy would be overwhelming at any age, but at just twenty-seven years old as was the case with Red, it is unfathomable. Unbeknownst to me before my trip, the plane crash not only impacted the university and its football program, but jolted the city of Huntington, as well. Perhaps no one was impacted more than Red. And, although it had been forty-four years later, and talk of the movie had faded somewhat since its release eight years before, and Red wasn't requested as much as before to be a guest speaker, I'd quickly learn that he was still very much identified with the tragedy that continued to impact a community. For example, on the day of my arrival, Red received a phone call for a request to be interviewed and videoed for a news report, and a call from an author who wanted to write a book on him. I was just in time!

Red welcomed me to his impressive home, and upon entering I immediately noticed six or seven boxes filled with lots of miscellaneous items, from tax returns to old bills to enough football-related items to fill a small museum. The boxes were likely the only items or space in the house not neatly organized. I distinctly recall Red saying, "If you get time, you can sort through these and probably find a few things which could be of help. Sorry I haven't organized the boxes, but I haven't looked through them in years—afraid some of what I would find might bring back some bad memories."

A "few" things? Red had kept *everything* beginning with his high school football career through his coaching tenure at Marshall. He told me someone once informed him long ago it was good to take notes during a meeting and if you weren't able to during the meeting itself, jot down everything you remembered from the meeting immediately after it. Red had notes on numerous meetings while at Marshall; based on these notes, it appeared that a number of these meetings had been host to some conflict. And the letters! Before my venture to Huntington, I only knew of "cc," or carbon copy, as something related to email. I learned there was a time when a copy of a letter could be duplicated by inserting a sheet of carbon between two sheets of paper. Red had saved every letter he had written while at Marshall via carbon copying, but it was the letters addressed to him that really got my attention, while giving me some sense of his character.

It's not surprising Red received numerous letters during the publicity the movie generated, nor that a number of Marshall players had written him. But, what I found most intriguing were the several letters from players who had quit the program, whether prior to the tragedy, after the tragedy, or even twice—before *and* after the plane crash. Granted, there were numerous individuals who left the program, many of whom thought practices were too tough. However, I was curious why several of them decided to write to Red, each of them giving reasons why they decided to leave, yet almost apologetic in nature for quitting.

Letters to Red soon after the tragedy included from Mode Stone, a longtime dean and athletics supporter at Florida State, who claimed, "No man in America has ever been confronted with a bigger task than you." A sportswriter for the *Tampa Tribune* recalled how coming out of Florida State, Red wanted to succeed so badly in the NFL, he told the writer even if they locked him in a room with then-Chicago Bears tight end and tough-guy Mike Ditka, Red would be the one emerging with the upper hand. In the wake of the tragedy, the writer added, "You've got to have that same kind of spirit now."

More recently, there was a letter from a Huntington businessman, who had just seen the movie, declaring, "You are my HERO. Thanks for being such a great person." There was another from a former Marshall baseball player, who had approached Red about a month prior to the crash in 1970, asking if he could also play football on scholarship and was turned down "for good reason," according to the player. He was writing to inform Red he "had made decisions then that allowed lives (including the former player) to go on." There was a letter from a pre-tragedy Marshall football player, who was writing to apologize for his father. His father, who had been thought of highly by the university, attempted to get Red fired after he had made his son run wind sprints at practice. About forty years later, the former player thanked Red, crediting him with making him "tougher."

Speaking of, there seemed to be an abundance of corroboration that Marshall football practices were tough back then, and Red was really tough, so much so that he once was questioned by McMullen for his "toughness."

"The whole staff was tough," Reggie Oliver told me in an interview. From Tuscaloosa, Alabama, Oliver was recruited by Red and was Marshall's starting quarterback the first three seasons after the tragedy. Interestingly, Oliver not only acknowledged Red as a fine defensive coach, but mentioned that with him calling the plays in 1971, Oliver was far less likely to throw an interception (6 in 177 attempts) than the two seasons (1972–1973) Red didn't call the plays

(29 in 385 attempts). "But, the staff, whether before the plane crash, and especially afterwards, was dealt with the *tough* task of trying to build the Marshall program. Red might have been tough, but he was more so fair."

Finally, there was a letter from a former player thanking Red for making the "movie come to fruition" and for giving him "the opportunity to play at Marshall." The player was severely injured "against Bowling Green late in the 1972 season," but Red and "Coach Lengyel" made sure he kept his scholarship for the entire four years although he was unable to play.

This particular letter prompted me to ask Red about the mysterious 1972 football season—one that Red was absolutely positive he did not coach but was working in construction by that time; however, all other records indicate otherwise. Months later and by the end of the book project, Red had been diagnosed with having repressed memory during that particular time. Some of those same bad memories Red wanted to avoid finding in the boxes had essentially been unconsciously blocked by him long ago, wiping out of his mind approximately a year's worth of Marshall and football.

I asked Red about the apparent friction between he and Coach Lengyel, McMullen, and other high-ranking staff members at Marshall. This prompted him to assert that although he wanted to be truthful, he didn't want to come across as being negative. For various reasons, he totally separated himself from Marshall for nearly twenty years. However, since Jim Donnan's arrival as head coach, followed by

Bobby Pruett, Mark Snyder, and now Doc Holliday, the Marshall coaching regimes have asked Red to be part of the program, and he has obliged. Red was reluctant at first, but now he cherishes this relationship with every ounce of his being.

I was very interested in determining why Donnan asked Red to be a part of the program, for if it wasn't for him asking, Red very well might still be separated from Marshall. Donnan said Keith Morehouse, currently the sports director of a news station in West Virginia and the radio play-by-play man of Thundering Herd games, first mentioned Red's name in 1990 as someone in the community who once had been involved with Marshall football. Donnan then discovered Red was the brother of Rhett Dawson, who had also played at Florida State and Donnan knew. "So, I found Red's number, called him up, and said, 'Look, I know it would be tough for you to be involved with the program, but I knew your brother and he can vouch for me,'" Donnan said. "I asked Red if we could meet, and if he could help me make some contacts in the community." Red explained to Donnan he hadn't been involved in a long time, and for good reason in his mind. "I said, 'Well, you don't have to be involved if you don't want to be. Let's just meet and get to know one another.'" Red and Donnan would eventually meet and, in time, Red became involved with Marshall football again.

As far as any indifference with certain individuals when he coached, Red admitted he and Lengyel certainly had their differences, but they have since made amends. As far as McMullen, they too certainly had their differences. "As far as what I thought of McMullen back then, remember, I don't want to be negative," Red said. "As far as what I think of him now, he passed away a long time ago. God rest his soul."

Red did comment about a high-ranking administrator he wanted to keep anonymous in the book. Although always attempting to think in a positive manner and trying to avoid recalling instances when he thought he was mistreated, Red brought up an incident from early March of 1971 when he was told by this administrator for no apparent reason that all the players stood up and applauded when informed that Red would not be Marshall's head coach. It's a story Red has always doubted but became curious about as we spoke about what really occurred. So, I spoke with a player from the '71 team and asked him about the incident.

"I don't remember it happening like that at all," said the anonymous player. "From what I remember, nothing was said about Red. What was said was Marshall was going to bring in a high-profiled coach with an identifiable name. When that was said, I think a few guys got up and clapped."

Red and I had discussed a lot of difficult things by the evening of our first day together. I had asked some tough questions, but he had been totally up front and honest. But, things were about to get even tougher. I asked him if he wanted to talk right then about the plane crash, its victims, what he witnessed, and the survivor's guilt he has endured ever since, or if he wanted to wait until after the following day's Fountain Ceremony. "Might as well do it now," he said. "But, first let me grab a couple of things to loosen up my tongue a bit." With that, he grabbed a beer and his can of Copenhagen.

As indicated, the following day's Fountain Ceremony was a phenomenal experience for me: emotional yet extraordinary and inspiring. As Red said, "If the memorial service doesn't move you, even if you know nothing about Marshall, something must be wrong with you." I wholeheartedly agree.

In front of what was described as the biggest crowd for the memorial that most could remember, speakers included President Stephen Kopp, who I would formally meet the next day. President Kopp would suddenly pass away only a little over a month later after ten years of moving the university light years ahead. Coach Holliday spoke, becoming emotional when he mentioned for the following day's game, the team would wear a "75" helmet decal for the second year in a row. Reacting to Holliday's emotion was the one time Red would tear up during the service, prompting him to later say in regard to a news reporter and a camera which followed him around for much of the weekend, "I hope that dang camera didn't get me crying!" Finally, the keynote speaker was Tommy Shoebridge, the middle of three brothers, the oldest having been Ted Shoebridge, the starting quarterback for Marshall in 1969 and 1970, and one of the seventy-five who perished in the plane crash. Tommy was most grateful for Marshall University and Huntington for keeping alive the memory of those who had died. Among others, he thanked Red in his speech for the continuous consoling of his mother, Yolanda, many times after Ted died. According to Tommy, Red's comfort and consoling words to his mother gave her the strength to allow her two younger sons to leave home after high school to pursue their educations after tragically losing her oldest son not long before.

After such an unbelievable experience, it was difficult to comprehend what was brought to my attention by one of Red's friends during my time in Huntington: two years before, a Marshall student wrote in the school newspaper, the *Parthenon*, a controversial column regarding the memorial service. Included in the column was the following: "Forty-two years have passed since these young athletes have died; why must we continue to be reminded [by the annual memorial service]? Or to put it more precisely, why must this display of pageantry continue? . . . The old cliché goes, 'Time heals all wounds.' Well, I say forty-two years is healing enough."

As expected, the column itself received much backlash but, from what I observed, its message was fully ignored. Still, for what it's worth, I'd like to counter with some statements from a few individuals I met at Marshall.

"After all these years, people still want to remember them," said Carl Kokor regarding the people involved in the tragedy. Kokor, now in his early eighties, was one of the three surviving Marshall coaches along with Red. And, according to Tommy Shoebridge, "I'm for anything that keeps their memories alive." Finally, to embody what the Fountain Ceremony means to most people who are aware of its significance—who desire for the "display of pageantry" to continue—I refer to an essay written by Patrick Keltry in response to the newspaper article. Patrick is part of the Marshall University College Program for Students with Autism Spectrum Disorder, and Red's good friend.

"When I see Coach at the ceremony, I see how it still pains him," Patrick said of Red and the tragedy, "but if he can be courageous and go on, I know I can continue to work hard and stay in school. . . . During the ceremony, I feel like each of the seventy-five are standing before me, smiling. I feel them with me all the time and when I feel like giving up, it's like they're all right there, encouraging me."

During my visit to Huntington, I was fortunate enough to really get to know a man who has meant a lot to a community and its people. Red Dawson is a tough and stern football coach-turned-construction worker, yet is passionate about poetry and is such a skilled and accomplished artist, his paintings are located in both the Valdosta (GA) High School and Marshall sports halls of fame. He is courteous, always tipping his hat to the ladies, and gladly signing every piece of memorabilia presented and posing for every photo requested—and, there were *a lot* of them. So much so, I would later say I felt like Red's one-man entourage, or his out-of-shape bodyguard, while we were out in public. But more so, Red is strength for some, and encouragement for others, while his heart, as *We Are Marshall* director McG claimed, has a lot to do with the foundation of the Huntington community and Marshall University.

For me, an outsider to the community, when I prepared to leave what had been my initial visit to a great town with genuine people, who make you feel like family, I hoped it wouldn't be my last. As I packed my car that Sunday afternoon, I could not keep the Fountain Ceremony from two days before off my mind. In case the speeches aren't moving enough, the memorial nears an end with a wreath set before the fountain, a name called, and a flower laid on the fountain for each of the seventy-five lives, and the fountain being silenced, not to be turned on until the spring.

"It's the moment when that water stops," Mickey Jackson started telling me in an interview while getting choked up, "that's symbolic of the moment the seventy-five heartbeats stopped on November 14, 1970." Along with Red and Kokor, Mickey is another one of the surviving coaches.

The service ended with a "We Are . . . Marshall" rallying cry. As I loudly responded "Marshall!" I did not feel like a visitor from Georgia, going through the motions, but actually part of the Marshall family, even if only the slightest because I had questioned whether I was deserving to be part of the "We." But then, I recalled something else Mickey had said: "We are all connected for life because of the memorial event, and it's our responsibility to continue this commitment and deliver the promise that we will never forget."

As I waved good-bye to my new friend, Red, he ran up to the car, motioning he had something to tell me before I left for home.

"One good thing that'll come out of us doing a book is by the time we're done, I bet you'll be a Marshall fan for life," he said. And I agreed. "Oh, and one other good thing. . ." he added. "By the time we're done, I also bet you will never, ever forget the seventy-five lives." And I certainly won't.

CHAPTER 1
NOT PERFECT—AND, FAR FROM IT

November 14, 1970, is etched in my mind forever. That day has been a significant part of me for forty-five years, and will be for as long as I live. And it's not for anything I *did* on that day, but for what I did *not* do. I did not board the Southern Airways flight bound for the Tri-State Airport in Wayne County, West Virginia. On board that plane were seventy of my closest friends, colleagues, and young men I had recruited and coached.

Over the years, I've been asked the same question countless times: can you tell me about the plane crash, or how did the plane crash affect you? My usual answer was no answer at all—I simply didn't talk about it. Or sometimes, I'd ask them to imagine, for just a moment, tragically losing seventy of their closest companions. That's essentially what happened to me on that November evening. And it happened in a flash, just like that.

I was just twenty-seven years old when what has been called both the greatest tragedy in college sports history, and the worst plane crash in the history of American sports, occurred on a short flight home from Greenville,

North Carolina, for seventy Marshall University football players, coaches, administrators, and boosters, and five members of the flight crew. I didn't know a whole lot at the time—only how to be a football coach—however, I quickly learned that because I was one of a few Marshall coaches and players spared from the tragedy, my life had been instantly changed forever.

It has been said I have experienced survivor's guilt, or survivor's syndrome, ever since the crash occurred. If the diagnosis of such a condition includes routinely having wished I had been on the plane with my friends, and experiencing nightmares that are absolutely hell—so bad that when I wake up from one, I dare not go back to sleep to avoid returning to the same nightmare—for decades, then, yes, I guess I do indeed suffer from survivor's guilt.

Fortunately for me, I have had a network—including my son, Bill Jr, and daughter, Katie—that has helped me handle this debilitating guilt. And, I'd be remiss if I didn't mention my ex-wife, Carole, who was nothing but great in dealing with my survivor's guilt for an awful long time. It's hard dealing with routinely waking up from a nightmare in a cold sweat—so much that the bedsheets would be soaked—but it's surely no piece of cake to be the one laying next to the person having the nightmare.

In addition, because of the tragedy and certain other stressful incidents I experienced soon after the crash, I've been diagnosed by so-called experts with repressed memory. I have always prided myself on having a good memory—a damn good one; however, I somehow "lost" about a year of my life, including the 1972 football season. For years, I believed I coached at Marshall for just one year after the crash, and claimed as much in interviews before it was pointed out within the last year that, in reality, I left the university after the '72 season, not 1971.

The fact I was not capable of detailing my memories of the crash changed significantly about ten years ago with the release of the Warner Bros. movie, *We Are Marshall.* The movie, where I am played by actor Matthew Fox, did wonders for Marshall University, and the great city where the school and I call home—Huntington, West Virginia. The film also brought attention to the plane crash while honoring its victims, which in turn meant that I was asked to give interviews and to speak to groups numerous times over a period of several years. Although hesitant to talk at first, I began to realize that the more I spoke about the crash, the more manageable my survivor's guilt became, and the fewer nightmares I had.

Even today, *We Are Marshall* continues to be a blessing for many people. For me, not only have the nightmares tapered off, but I am fully mindful that if *We Are Marshall* never happened, you probably wouldn't be reading a book about me because it is likely I would not be involved in a book deal. But, be that as it may, I'm going to take full advantage of this humbling opportunity. Besides detailing the crash and my survivor's guilt, I discuss, in the following pages, some personally discouraging circumstances involving Marshall and its football program leading up to and soon following the tragedy—incidents that, until now, I've been hesitant to talk about.

Every November 14 on the university campus, the Fountain Ceremony is held honoring the seventy-five victims of the plane crash. Since the Memorial Student Center Fountain was dedicated to the victims, I've hardly missed a ceremony, although I was well hidden and unable to be seen for most of the annual gatherings.

For decades, I attended the Fountain Ceremony by myself. I would park far from the fountain, and far away from everyone else. I walked past Old Main, the historic administrative building, approaching the ceremony from the back where a sycamore tree stood. There, I would stand right beside the tree, sometimes behind it, cutting a single notch in it every year with a knife I carried. Since the ceremony was held at night back then, I was basically completely hidden from view.

I wasn't trying to hide from paying respect to those who perished, but rather I simply didn't want to talk to anyone, and didn't want anyone talking to me. If I attended the ceremony in the same manner as everyone else, I would've had to engage with people about the one thing I didn't want to even *think* about—the plane crash and its victims. I was a very emotional person—still am—and any conversation I had related to the tragedy resulted in what I've dreaded for most of my life: becoming emotional in public, which is really embarrassing for me.

Just prior to the start of the Fountain Ceremony in 2005, and only months after he became the president of

Marshall, the late Stephen Kopp spotted me at the sycamore, walked over, and asked if I'd like to join him during the service. As politely and respectfully as I could, I turned him down: "I'm pretty comfortable right here by this tree, Steve." However, toward the end of the ceremony, I found myself not getting ready to leave the tree and hurrying back to my car like I had always done before, but wandering toward the crowd, whereupon I stood at the back of all the onlookers.

For the following year's ceremony, what had once been the unthinkable occurred: I was asked to be the keynote speaker, and I actually accepted. Granted, *We Are Marshall* had been in production for over a year, and would be released in just over a month, so I had plenty of practice speaking to the media about the tragedy. But, I had yet to speak in front of a large group.

In the end, despite keeping myself under control for the most part, it was difficult getting through my speech and I got a little embarrassed because I became somewhat emotional. However, because of where I spoke and who I spoke to—in front of a friendly Marshall crowd—the experience wasn't bad at all.

Ironically, the sycamore I once stood by has disappeared. I'm not sure if it blew down in a storm or was taken down purposely. At recent ceremonies, I have taken a seat amongst my people.

I MENTIONED I DID not like becoming emotional in public. Although I've gotten somewhat used to it lately, getting emotional publicly is still a fear of mine to some degree, especially when it could also indicate a lack of toughness on my part. As a boy growing up in Valdosta, Georgia, I assumed I had to be macho—the toughest guy in the fight. And, even after many years, it's difficult to lose that persona, abandon that mentality.

The desire to be tough began at the beginning of seventh grade when a certain Bobby and his chum Jimmy would get me on the ground at recess and start beating on me. This happened nearly every school day, for two solid years, and always in front of the girls—it was embarrassing, and because of it, I thought I'd never get a girlfriend!

I had seen the Charles Atlas ads in boys' magazines, calling for "Skinny" or the "Weakling," who just lost his girlfriend to the bully, to send away for Atlas's free book to gain muscle. He then would beat up the bully and win back the girlfriend. Although I didn't quite need to send off for his book to tell me what I needed to do to no longer be bullied, Charles Atlas helped me recognize I was tired of getting pushed around.

Though Charles Atlas mentally prepared me for emotional toughness, I still needed to bulk up physically, and thanks to my dad, I was able to do so. One day, my old man went out to a junkyard and returned with a car axle and two large tin cans. He placed the cans on both ends of the axle and poured lead into them, making a makeshift barbell. Sonny Shroyer, who would later be better known as Enos on the CBS series *The Dukes of Hazzard*, lived less than a block away, and he showed me how I could curl the barbell, press it, and do squats and shoulder raises (and here, I can now barely raise my arms above my shoulders). Sonny soon had "Little Brother," as he called me, working out relentlessly all the time. Soon, after a few trips by my daddy to the junkyard, my two brothers and I had a backyard-turned-weight room filled with salvaged parts-turned-weight room equipment. As they say, one man's trash is another man's treasure.

By obsessively lifting weights and gaining a great deal of confidence, I became a much different kid than the one who got beat up at recess. (As far as Bobby and Jimmy, they quickly went from bullies to a couple of piss ants. Still, I credit them for laying the groundwork for me becoming one tough son of a gun.) In just two years after being constantly bullied, I was crowned "King Ugly" of the school; despite the name, it was actually a popularity contest. Soon thereafter, I was a starting offensive and defensive end on the football team. And, there was a notion that if you became a starter for the Valdosta Wildcats, you were assured of success for the rest of your life—at least, that's what I was led to believe, and for good reason, given the program's history.

Because of its successful football history, Valdosta has been recognized as "Winnersville" and "TitleTown USA," or simply put, the city *is* football. With a population size similar to that of Huntington, around 50,000, it is home to America's winningest football team—the Valdosta High School Wildcats, whose all-time win total is approaching 900. There is a sign reminding you of such as you enter the city limits. Under head coach Wright Bazemore, I grew up during Valdosta's heyday. It's been forty-five years since Coach Bazemore coached his final game, but his career winning percentage still ranks in the top five or six in Georgia high school football history. To get an idea of how dominant Valdosta was back then, here's a stat: the Wildcats have captured a Georgia-record 23 state championships in its entire history, and 14 of those were won in just a 25-season period from the late 1940s through the early 1970s.

At eleven years old, I'll never forget when the Jesup Yellow Jackets defeated Valdosta toward the end of the 1954 season, stopping the Wildcats' 38-game non-losing streak. Like a lot of young boys in Valdosta, I was absolutely distraught that night, thinking the world might actually come to an end. The Wildcats weren't supposed to lose! It seemed every boy growing up in Valdosta back then lived and died by the Wildcats, and wanted desperately to eventually play for them. Most boys started off down the path to play for Valdosta. Many of these aspiring Wildcats, however, would soon be looking for something new to do after school after encountering Coach Bazemore, his staff, and their physically and mentally rough practices.

ALTHOUGH I ALWAYS THOUGHT it was probably because they couldn't remember my name, Coach Bazemore and his staff started calling me "Red," supposedly because of my red-colored hair (for what it's worth, the red has been gone for a while now, and maybe it's about time to change my name to "Whitey"). Coach Bazemore was a hell of a coach, a hell of a motivator, highly respected, but very tough. Still, his assistant coaches could be even tougher.

"Red, you ought to get somebody to pee on you, so at least you'd smell like a man!" was a particular assistant's outburst I especially remember. Another expression often used by a different assistant coach: "Red, you're standing around like a bottle full of stale urine!" What is now considered verbal abuse, and wouldn't be tolerated, was just how it was back then, how I grew up—how I learned to be a better football player.

Nowadays, some states' high school sports associations regulate how many intrasquad scrimmages its football teams can conduct. I'm guessing there were no such regulations back then because Coach Bazemore had us scrimmaging on Monday, Tuesday, Wednesday, and sometimes Thursday; we played on Friday, and if we didn't play well, we scrimmaged on Saturday too.

Only once in almost thirty years as Valdosta's head coach did Coach Bazemore, who passed away in 1999, have back-to-back seasons of what would be considered average teams, and I was a part of them: 1958 and 1959, my junior and senior years. By then, I had realized Valdosta couldn't be perfect every season, the world didn't come to an end when the Wildcats lost, and it was no fun scrimmaging on most Saturdays.

It was with this mentality that I continued to pursue football, now at the college level. During my senior year at

Valdosta, I was fortunate to receive recruiting letters from several southern football teams, including some big-time programs—like the team I grew up idolizing, the Georgia Tech Yellow Jackets—requesting that I visit their school.

My older brother, Jack Jr. and I worshiped the Georgia Tech football team. We had all the players' names memorized for several of their teams during the early 1950s. I can still recite most of the names from Tech's perfect, 12–0 Sugar Bowl squad of 1952. So, you could say I was dealt quite a blow when Georgia Tech didn't offer me a scholarship because I was "too small," as they claimed. The University of Georgia said the same thing. In fact, once all those teams that had invited me for a visit got a good look at my tall but very skinny 175-pound frame, and figured out that I wasn't all that fast either, only two schools offered me a scholarship: Western Carolina and Florida State. And surely, I believed, the scouts from those two schools sent to Valdosta must have gotten me confused with some other player: perhaps they had wanted to give a scholarship to jersey number 48, but mistakenly offered it to number 47.

I decided to attend Florida State due in large part to my fondness for Perry Moss, who would be entering his second season in 1960 as the head coach of the Seminoles, but also because I was told by someone very close to me that I would never make it at a "big school" like Florida State. And, when I was challenged, I usually tried to tackle it.

Florida State didn't quite have the reputation it has today—not even close. The school was only a little over a decade removed from being an all-girls college. Doak Campbell, FSU's football stadium, held less than 20,000 at capacity. Plus, the football program had just recently begun playing upper-tier competition—games that almost inevitably ended in defeat—including the University of Florida, who would play the Seminoles only on its home field in Gainesville.

After signing with Florida State partly because of the head coach, I arrived in Tallahassee only to be informed that Perry Moss had left the program. After just one year at FSU, Coach Moss headed north to become the general manager and head coach of the Montreal Alouettes of the Canadian Football League. Bill Peterson, who had been an assistant at LSU, was the Seminoles' new head coach. Since this was before freshmen were allowed to play varsity ball, I would first be under the direction of head freshman coach Charlie LaPradd. Coach LaPradd had been an All-American lineman at Florida and was tough, intimidating, and apparently didn't think too much of me as a player.

In turn, I was going to have to seek inspiration from elsewhere if I wanted to believe I could remain a tough member of the team and avoid letting my emotions get the best of me. Thus, as I often had growing up as an active member of Valdosta's Christ Episcopal Church, and later an FCA (Fellowship of Christian Athletes) camp leader for several summers, I decided to turn to the Old Master (as I prefer to call my Heavenly Father).

One of the first steps was my decision to be part of the roughly 15,000 to see evangelist Billy Graham speak at

Doak Campbell Stadium during my freshman year. Walking out of the stadium that night, I thought to myself, by God, I'm tough enough—I'm buying into this, and am "all in" to what Billy Graham preached! And, when I was all in into doing something, I wanted to do it perfectly. It was obvious I wasn't the perfect football player, as Coach LaPradd often reminded me. But, I could be perfect *morally* by following the gospel to the fullest extent, and spreading its word to others.

Alas, it didn't take long before I realized I could not possibly be without sin, and the countless tan coeds from South Florida that surrounded me had a lot to do with that. Walking around campus, I soon discovered there were many other girls to admire than just my girlfriend at the time. I distinctly recall a couple of times literally turning away from a passing, beautiful and bouncing girl, praying that the impure thoughts would leave my mind. As simple and silly as it sounds, having dirty thoughts about a bunch of girls at FSU, is what ultimately convinced me that I am not, nor is anyone else, perfect—not then, not now.

One decision that I've made since the 1970 crash that was less than perfect was my decision to hold a grudge against certain individuals affiliated with the university for years—make that, decades.

Immediately after a three- to four-month recruiting period that followed the plane crash, some Marshall academic and athletic administrators suddenly made me feel—and, maybe it was my imagination at the time—like they'd be better off without me and the other surviving assistant coaches, Mickey Jackson and Carl Kokor. Graduate assistant Gail Parker, who was riding with me when we heard the news of the crash, was eventually dismissed altogether. I coached for two more seasons, angry at seemingly everyone: the new head coach, Jack Lengyel; athletic director Joe McMullen; other Marshall administrators; and even certain sportswriters who covered the team when I discovered they had printed some things about me that just weren't accurate.

Even after leaving the university, I unfortunately remained angry at Marshall. But, sometime during the 1990s, the place that once made me feel like they'd be better off without me actually reached out, wanting me to be part of the school and football program again.

At first, I was hesitant to reconnect with Marshall, but I then realized that my anger was hurting no one but myself, and not helping anyone. What's more, I found that besides trying to overcome my "survivor's guilt," I had spent a lot of time overwhelmed with frustration and being mad at people, and I was absolutely mentally exhausted!

Now, I no longer hold any grudges, and have made good with a number of the people that I once was distant from, like Jack Lengyel. I love Marshall. The university and football program have been very good to me, and for that, I'm forever grateful.

Besides the plane crash, or how it has affected me, probably the questions I get asked the most are related to if I'm still scared to fly, and whose fault was it that the plane crashed.

Contrary to some reports that came out just days after the Marshall plane crash, I'm actually not afraid to fly. As I see it, if the Old Master decides to come for you, he can get you if you're flying in a plane, riding in a car, as I sit here writing this book—whenever. As far as what caused the plane to crash, there were some reports that the NTSB (National Transportation Safety Board) almost declared it was pilot error over instrument failure. However, an "official" cause could never be found.

My opinion is this—even today, utilizing the best in aviation technology, it's not the smoothest of rides into the Tri-State Airport. Passing the Ashland oil refinery in Kentucky, over a ridge of trees aligning West Virginia Route 75—the same trees the Marshall plane clipped—flights approach the airport real high and then there is a sudden drop while passing over a wooded hillside—where the Marshall plane nosedived after clipping the trees—to reach a runway that is essentially located on top of a mountain. Forty-five years after the crash, the average passenger will get all pinched up inside as the plane drops towards the runway. Back in 1970, it was even more of an adventure—"like landing on an aircraft carrier," I recall a pilot saying in the newspaper after the crash.

At the time of the crash, and unlike today, Tri-State didn't have a glidescope instrument landing system which would have warned the plane it was flying too low to clear the ridges before the runway. The airport desperately wanted a glidescope, but couldn't have one installed because of the costs involved in constructing the system, expenses which financially-strapped Huntington would have had to partially pay.

A plane being flown at night in rainy and foggy weather, like it was on November 14, 1970, into an airport with no glidescope system, would have had a damn difficult time landing. Add in the fact that the plane's captain, Frank Abbott, had neither landed nor taken off at Tri-State. Thus, the airport became "where a crash is bound to happen," said a member of an airport safety committee right after the tragedy.

So, who's at fault for the Marshall plane crash? Personally, I don't know if it was anyone's fault. Besides, it really wouldn't matter to me if someone or something was to blame; the tragedy regrettably occurred, and it unfortunately can never be undone.

Finally, another question I'm likely to hear going forward is why am I doing this—writing a book? Frankly, though it might sound selfish, one of the reasons that I agreed to write a book is so I can continue to heal. The *We Are Marshall* movie and talking about the tragedy really helped with the guilt and shame I carry, while decreasing the nightmares, but I'm far from completely healed. I thought putting my words to paper might provide a little extra relief.

More so, I held negative thoughts against Marshall for an awfully long time, and although this grudge may have only been evident in my mind, I want the admiration I now have for Marshall to be fully demonstrated. The university and its football program deserve at least that much for how good they've been to me.

But most of all, I want to pay tribute to all the people, most of whom were friends of mine, who perished on the one day etched in my mind forever, by recounting, in my own words, the truthful and sometimes brutally honest story of Marshall football: from failure and probation to the plane crash to the untold account of the in-house turmoil that persisted as we tried to rebuild a football program. The seventy-five individuals involved in the greatest tragedy in college sports history laid that foundation of triumph, and each and every one of them should never be forgotten—ever.

CHAPTER 2
HEY, YOU GOT ANY RED MAN?

AFTER PLAYING PRIMARILY ON defense for the Florida State Seminoles as a sophomore in 1962, I began a new role as a junior the next year, when I also played offensive end. Entering the same season, head coach Bill Peterson was in need of someone to fill the role of ends/receivers coach, and fast. Without even meeting him first, Coach Peterson asked a Birmingham, Alabama, native to interview for the open position. This "Little" All-American from just over a decade before at Birmingham's Howard College (now Samford University) was fresh off a head coaching stint at Howard, where he dominated Alabama small-college football. He easily got the job at Florida State.

Our newly-hired position coach, a thirty-four-year-old named Bobby Bowden, immediately started calling me "just a good ole country boy from Georgia," which I found ironic given his own southern roots. I quickly became really fond of Coach Bowden, who had as much of a way with words in the mid-1960s as he would be known for decades later. My favorite expression of Coach Bowden's was his opinion of a football player who was said to have "potential": "A boy that has potential means he ain't done it yet."

During all the years I've known Coach Bowden, probably the happiest I've ever seen him was when he was riding a two-man blocking sled in practice. In the two years he was my position coach, I was often one of the two men pushing him around the practice field. Coach Bowden would giggle and chuckle as he rode the sled for what must have been at least fifty combined miles during my junior and senior seasons. I swear, throughout my time at Florida State, Coach Bowden and I must have worn out two of those sleds.

Also, almost daily without fail at practice, I'd hear somebody yelling, "Dawson! Dawson! Dawson!" I'd look up, and here would come Coach Bowden heading directly at me, and just a hollering. He'd never cuss at me, but he often shouted his familiar "ding dang-it," "dog gone-it," "dern it," or "dag nabb-it." Coach Bowden would reach up and grab the area of my shoulder pads surrounding my neck and yank me over to one side away from the rest of the players, who surely thought I was really in for it. He would then grab my helmet through its ear holes, pulling my head down to where we were seeing eye to eye. Suddenly, his hollering lowered to a soft, near-whisper, and then he'd mutter just a few inches away from my face, "Hey, you got any Red Man?"

Yet the arrival of Coach Bowden and my new role on the team weren't the only changes that FSU football experienced that year. Another quite prominent change was the introduction of Coach Peterson's passing offense. Coach Bowden would be one of the first to admit that he was one of our assistants who doubted Peterson's passing offense when it was introduced. Nevertheless, with a pro-style passing philosophy, the head coach would pretty quickly bring the Seminoles to the forefront of college football.

After being defeated by Houston 28-8, when Florida State passed for less than 100 yards and scored its only touchdown on an interception return, to end a losing 1961 season, the Seminoles opened the 1962 campaign during my sophomore year (my first year on the varsity), against The Citadel. Armed to the hilt, we routed the Bulldogs 49-0, and broke a school record for single-game total yardage, including nearly 300 yards passing. We used two quarterbacks, Eddie Feely, a five-foot-seven senior, and Steve Tensi, a six-foot-five sophomore from Cincinnati. Tensi was the tallest quarterback in the country and had chosen FSU over about 70 schools. That night, Tensi and Feely must have completed passes to about 10 different guys. Even I caught one for a short gain.

Besides adopting an innovative passing attack, it was around this time that FSU's football program also started improving its facilities (Doak Campbell more than doubled its seating capacity in just four years), signing better players, and facing better opponents, while even beating some of them.

It was also about this time I was given a recording of a Florida State coaching clinic during Perry Moss's one year in Tallahassee. The clinic's speaker was Ray Eliot, who had just finished a head-coaching career at Illinois of nearly twenty years. Moss had been a quarterback on one of Eliot's two Rose Bowl–winning Illinois teams. Eliot's "football philosophy," as it is called, is a powerful, and emotional speech about how everything, including one's approach to playing football, starts in one's mind: it's a "mental" game as much as anything else. As Eliot says, "if you think you can do it, you can." Even today, I can still recite Eliot's speech word for word—all twenty-four-plus minutes of it. I'll often pop in my DVD of the speech while driving. I swear, after listening for only a few minutes, I feel like pulling my car over, and seeking out a tree to tackle.

Midway through the 1962 season, we had a record of 2-1-1, which included a scoreless tie at Kentucky and a 7-6 loss against a top-10 Miami team in the Orange Bowl. Next up was another reputable opponent on the road, Georgia, who had defeated Florida State 42-0 the last time the two met in Athens three years earlier. The Bulldogs were favored to hand us another setback, but in a way, unknowingly following Ray Eliot's football philosophy, we actually thought we would upset Georgia before even setting foot on the field.

The players weren't the only ones who smelled an upset. Dr. Coyle Moore was Dean of the School of Social Welfare at Florida State, and heavily involved in Seminole athletics, including serving on the athletic committee for a number of years. I personally knew Dr. Moore as someone who always gave me great advice, a good guy, and (even though it seemed every other word out of his mouth was "hell") a true gentleman.

I'll never forget what Dr. Moore said to me right before we left to play Georgia in Athens: "Now, when we beat

Georgia, I want you to somehow get a piece of their turf from the goal line and bring it back to me." It instantly struck me that he said "*when* we beat Georgia," not "*if*"—a word I try to avoid using. Where I come from, we have a saying about the word "if": *if* the dog hadn't stopped to take a shit, he would have caught the rabbit. Dr. Moore didn't say *what* he planned on doing with the turf, only to bring him back a piece.

We led the Bulldogs only 3-0 late in the third quarter until we tacked on two touchdowns for an 18-0 victory. Besides me pulling a plug of Georgia's turf from one of their goal lines, what I recall most about the memorable win was twofold—the first was the incredible play of two of my teammates, Charlie Calhoun and Keith Kinderman, who would become lifelong friends of mine; and the second was my search for a long-lost girlfriend.

Coach Peterson mimicked LSU's three-team system of platooning players (known as the Chinese Bandits), where the 11-player units were instead known at FSU as the Chiefs, the Renegades, and the Warriors. The Chiefs normally played a little more than half the game on offense and defense. The Renegades were the backup defensive unit, and the Warriors the backup offensive unit. Listed as a six-foot-three, 215-pound end, I was a member of the Renegades in 1962, as was safety Charlie Calhoun.

Members of the same freshman team, Charlie was also like me in that he wasn't regarded as much of a great player initially, but he would wind up with a pretty good varsity career at FSU. Originally a quarterback, he was moved to the defensive backfield where he excelled, and he was also our primary punter for three seasons. In the win over Georgia, Charlie punted a bunch of times, keeping the Bulldogs on their far end of the field for most of the game. He also totaled about a half-dozen tackles, including one where he laid out a Bulldog receiver at midfield after he caught a pass, resulting in a fumble, which we recovered.

Keith Kinderman, a starting halfback on the Chiefs unit, was a bruising, tough runner, who was also a threat to catch the ball out of the backfield. As he did for the entire 1961 season, his first at FSU after transferring from Iowa, Keith was the leader of a strong rushing attack in our shutout at Georgia. For the season, he would lead the team in receiving.

I had a pretty good game in Athens, as well: made one interception, recovered one fumble, caught one pass, and pulled one plug of turf. But, I soon had my sights set on a hopeful, post-game reunion with my Rosie.

Rosie had been a girlfriend of mine when we were younger, and we continued to be close friends during high school. When we went our separate ways for college—she to the University of Georgia—Rosie and I corresponded a little at first by writing letters. Although we hadn't spoken to one another for some time, I knew she was still attending Georgia and, for some reason, was absolutely positive she would have gone to the game, and would be waiting for me outside the visitor's dressing room. So, after grabbing the sod, I raced into the dressing room, showered real good, and put on my coat and tie. Alas, I searched all over, but never saw Rosie.

Years later, I jokingly asked Rosie why the hell she didn't come see me after the '62 FSU-Georgia game, and she had a good excuse: she couldn't have come even if she had wanted to—Rosie was married.

Upon our return to Tallahassee, I did what I promised and brought the piece of Sanford Stadium's sod to Dr. Moore. He held on to it for a little while before burying it north of Doak Campbell next to the practice fields. This was the start of FSU's "Sod Cemetery," which has become one of the Seminoles' greatest football traditions.

Having gained a considerable amount of weight, which put me up to 230 pounds, I was on the Chiefs unit as a junior in 1963, starting on both offense and defense. We opened up against Miami again in the Orange Bowl as more than a touchdown underdog, and having lost to the Hurricanes eight times in the series' nine-game history.

The Seminoles defenders would be facing the strong-armed George Mira, who had finished in the top 10 of the Heisman Trophy voting the season before. In his last game, Mira had passed for about 325 yards against Nebraska in freezing temperatures at Yankee Stadium's Gotham Bowl. At the end of the 1963 season, Mira would add another top-10 Heisman Trophy finish and was a top-15 pick in the NFL Draft, but it wasn't because of his performance against Florida State. Against us, he did not complete his first pass until just before halftime, finished with two interceptions, and couldn't guide Miami to a single score in a 24-0 shutout!

Of course, we also had the advantage of having Fred Biletnikoff on our team. Everyone at Florida State knew Fred Biletnikoff was a special player. Maybe we didn't initially think he was as special as someone who would eventually be inducted into both the College and Pro Football Hall of Fames. Heck, the trophy that goes to the best wide receiver in college football is named after him! But, we knew he was definitely special.

Before he played a single down of varsity ball, Biletnikoff was already being called maybe the best pass receiver in FSU history. However, he missed the first half of the 1962 season after fracturing his foot just a little over a week before our season opener against The Citadel, and didn't get to fully display his talents the final five games that year. Against Miami and Mira, Biletnikoff was on full display, scoring all three of our touchdowns: two on the receiving end from Tensi, and an interception of Mira he returned for a 99-yard score.

Overall, a 1963 season that began with a lot of promise finished with a few close, but frustrating losses. Never having defeated Georgia Tech, Auburn, or Florida, we were beaten again by all three in November of that year, but by an average of only a touchdown.

Chosen 148th overall by the AFL's Boston Patriots in late November, and 161st overall by the Los Angeles Rams of the NFL in December, I was the only Seminole selected in either of the two professional football drafts in the 1964 off-season. As a "future" pick, I was chosen even though I had a year of eligibility remaining because I had been part of the 1960 incoming class four years before (I was redshirted for a season). Therefore, a drafted player could leave college following a fourth-year junior season—and, some guys did so—but I'm sure glad I stuck around for what many call the season that put FSU football on the map.

In 1964, the unlimited substitution rule was adopted in the college game, essentially resulting in two-platoon football. Instantly, our Chiefs-Renegades-Warriors platooning units were history, and there were basically no more double-dippers in college ball playing on both offense and defense. This could hinder a team, or help one like ours, in need of guys solely on offense for a complicated pro-style attack.

That year, Coach Peterson wanted to pass the ball even more than before, like about 10 more attempts per game, when we had been averaging roughly 17 passes per contest. This in itself was already a lot, especially in the three-yards-and-a-cloud-of-dust offensive region of the Deep South. Peterson hoped that his planned pass-even-more attack would not only support an offense that threw the ball all over the field, but would also attract more highly-touted recruits to Florida State, more fans, and a particular former assistant of the head coach.

When Coach Peterson arrived at Florida State, he asked Bill Crutchfield, a one-time assistant under Peterson at Mansfield Senior High School in Ohio and former head coach at Presbyterian College, to join him in Tallahassee. However, Crutchfield decided to take a job at the University of Miami. By 1964, at a time when we were facing better opposition (and had even routed Miami the season before), Coach Crutchfield became our offensive coordinator.

It was said the outside hire of Crutchfield caused some dissension among the assistants already in place, which included some of the very best coaches in the game. Besides Coach Bowden, who would become one of the greatest football coaches in history, legendary Don James (Washington) and John Coatta (Wisconsin) both became head coaches of big-time programs. Additionally, Bob Harbison became an FSU athletics icon, coaching the Seminoles for thirty-seven of the football program's first thirty-nine years. Despite the possibility of dissension amongst the coaches, the team, nevertheless, had great results on the field.

Playing what would now be considered a tight end position, I almost led the team in receiving as a junior, while being named by the media to the first-team All-Florida college team. But, in 1964, although we threw the ball more, adding an additional wideout in senior Donnie Floyd, I was used more as a blocking end than a receiver, lining up right next to my buddy, tackle Tom West. More so than him being a tad bit taller than me at six-foot-four, I was always looking up to Tom, and have done so for more than fifty years, and with good reason. After being heavily involved in the ROTC at Florida State, Tom would eventually reach the rank of major general in the Air Force before his retirement.

With Biletnikoff and I serving as co-captains of the team, we again opened the season on the road in the Orange Bowl with a shutout over Miami. Again, Biletnikoff scored all the game's touchdowns, coming on two passes from Tensi, in a 14-0 win. In fact, led by a magnificent front seven, rightfully called the "Magnificent Seven" or the "Seven Magnificents"—Frank Pennie, Avery Sumner, George D'Alessandro, Jack Shinholser, Max Wettstein, Bill McDowell, and Dick Herman—and a secondary known as the "Forgotten Four," the Seminoles' defense shut out the first three opponents we faced. But, the defense's best performance may have come in our fourth game in a highly-anticipated meeting with the University of Kentucky on homecoming.

Kentucky was another team FSU had never defeated in its history. The Wildcats were fresh off wins over No. 7 Auburn and top-ranked Ole Miss the week before. Coach Charley Bradshaw's team was ranked No. 5 in the nation (I believe the program hasn't been ranked as high since). The Dunkel Index—a sports rating system recognized as "the most accurate sports index since 1929"—had selected Kentucky as an overwhelming favorite to defeat us. However, on an unusually hot afternoon in mid-October, the most accurate index wasn't accurate at all.

With temperatures in the 80s, we jumped on Kentucky quickly, leading 21-0 by the end of the opening quarter. Around that time, I distinctly recall looking across the field at the Wildcats' sideline and, even though there was still a lot of football left to be played, thinking "It's over!"

as I saw several of their players throwing up. In venturing 650 miles south, Kentucky had been totally unprepared for the Tallahassee heat, and we would no doubt be able to cruise the rest of the way. Coasting to a 48-6 win, the FSU defense held the Wildcats to less than one yard per rushing attempt, allowed just one-third of their passes to be completed (11 of 33), and was pitching a shutout until yielding a garbage touchdown with less than 30 seconds left in the game. It supposedly remains one of the biggest upsets in college football history, according to the Dunkel Index.

After we had defeated NC State to improve to 7-1-1 in mid-November, two representatives from the Gator Bowl met with FSU athletic director Vaughn Mancha and Coach Peterson to discuss the possibility that we'd be invited to their bowl prior to the following week's regular-season finale against Florida. However, no overnight invitation was given and the Gator Bowl insisted on a victory over the Gators before a bid would be extended. It certainly wasn't the first time we felt our football program had not been fully respected.

There was a time during the 1950s that the University of Florida actually thought it was far superior to Florida State—the former all-girls school—on the football field, and thus would not play FSU. In the middle of the decade, a bill was actually voted down in the state legislature for the two schools to face one another until Florida Governor LeRoy Collins personally requested the University of Florida president to schedule a yearly series between the two programs. The series started in 1958 but was played only in Gainesville for the first six years (Florida having a 5-0-1 series advantage) until our stadium was enlarged to hold over 40,000.

In my final regular-season game, the Gators were coming to Tallahassee and, like the Seminoles, were also nationally ranked in the top 15. Yet, they still apparently had little respect for us. We had heard that during the week Florida players wore stickers on their helmets in practice reading "Never, FSU, Never," as if the Seminoles would never beat the Gators. And then, when we—senior guard Dick Hermann, Bitletnikoff, Tensi, and myself—went out for the coin toss, we saw the Gators had a big "Go For Seven" stitched across the top of the front of their jerseys, as if they were going for seven games in the series history without a loss to Florida State.

In preparing for Florida, the FSU coaches decided to throw a wrinkle into our offense by lining me up at fullback for the majority of our offensive plays—the only time as a Seminole I played a position on offense other than end. This change in formation gave us an extra man in the backfield to block, allowing Tensi additional time to throw against the Gators' quick, blitzing defensive line. The offensive ploy seemed to really confuse Florida and we took advantage of it.

After a scoreless first quarter, Tensi found Biletnikoff for a long, 50-something-yard touchdown, giving FSU a 7-0 lead, which we held at halftime. It would be one of just two catches for Biletnikoff, who was often double- and even triple-teamed by the Gators. This left a wide-open Floyd, who caught seven of the team's 11 completions.

In the second half, two field goals by FSU's Les Murdock were answered with a touchdown run by a particular Gator quarterback who would remain in the national spotlight for the next half-century and beyond—Steve Spurrier. That season, senior quarterback Tom Shannon would sometimes start, like he did against us, but Spurrier, who was only a sophomore, was quickly inserted into each game. It was a fumble lost by Spurrier that led to the Tensi-to-Biletnikoff touchdown.

Trailing 13-7 with more than nine minutes left in the game, the Gators did something kind of foolish by deciding to try an onside kick, which we recovered on Florida's side of the field. Just over two minutes later, Murdock kicked his third field goal to essentially clinch what had been an elusive victory over the Gators, 16-7.

Notably, our offense in 1964 could hardly be stopped, ranking in the nation's top 10 in passing and total offense. Our team's defense was probably even better, ranking in the nation's top 10 in total defense, rushing defense, and scoring defense, but not enough could be said about kicker Les Murdock.

A big guy at six-foot-two and about 230 pounds, besides placekicker, Murdock was also listed as a fullback, although I don't think he ever carried the ball as a Seminole. In a time when few teams had a player who solely kicked, Murdock, who entered his senior season of 1964 having made only one career field goal, attempted more field goals against Florida (five) than our opponents tried against us the entire season (four). Like our offense that season, FSU was also rather innovative in having an offensive weapon in Les, who made nine field goals for the season, including three against the Gators.

Following Murdock's third three-pointer, Florida, trailing by nine points, had two more shots on offense. Both possessions ended in Spurrier being intercepted. The Gators' quest for "Never, FSU, Never" was no more, while their "Go For Seven" was halted at six.

The Gator Bowl finally extended a bid to us and, contingent on a victory over Georgia in its final regular-season game, Georgia Tech appeared to be our opponent. This would have especially been a thrill for me to play and probably beat the team I grew up idolizing in my final collegiate game. However, Tech lost to the Bulldogs, so we were paired with Oklahoma, who had only a 6-3-1 record, but were ranked No. 2 early in the season and were riding a six-game streak without a loss.

In front of what was then a Gator Bowl-record crowd of over 50,000, we routed the Sooners, 36-19, and it wasn't even that close. In what was their final collegiate games Tensi passed for over 300 yards, while Biletnikoff unbelievably had almost 200 yards receiving on 13 catches. Oklahoma, who had entered with the fifth-best rushing offense in the nation, couldn't even average two yards per carry (74 yards on 42 rushes), while nearly half of the Sooners' passing yardage came on a single play, a 95-yard touchdown pass when we were comfortably ahead in the final quarter. About the only thing that didn't go right in the Gator Bowl was our place-kicking situation.

A couple of days prior to the game, it was announced Les was ineligible to play. Come to find out, he had enrolled at Tampa University in 1959, and although he didn't play football or was credited with any course work because he promptly left Tampa after a roofing accident, Murdock was declared to have used up all his eligibility. As far as our placekicker for the Gator Bowl, we essentially didn't have one. After halfback Phil Spooner, who led us in rushing that season, missed the first PAT try of the game, we attempted two-point conversions following our next four touchdowns—all no good. With victory well in hand, Phil was sent out to try the PAT after our sixth and final touchdown—another miss. The Gator Bowl proved to me how valuable a reliable placekicker, like Les Murdock, could be to a team!

Not long after graduating and leaving Florida State, I began my professional football career with the Boston Patriots—a team quarterbacked by "Kentucky Babe," Babe Parilli. Parilli, in his mid-thirties, had led Boston to a 10-3-1 record in 1964 after reaching the AFL title game the season before. Despite having been a relatively late-round pick, the coaching staff believed I could see significant playing time at linebacker, tight end, or maybe both positions. And, I did play, and played well—at least, during the exhibition season.

In my first game, a preseason exhibition against the Buffalo Bills, I intercepted the eventual Republican Party nominee in 1996 for Vice President, the late Jack Kemp, in my own end zone. By the final exhibition game against the

Kansas City Chiefs, I was starting at left linebacker. However, that's about it—the highlights of my NFL career!

By the start of the *real* 1965 NFL season, I was backing up Jack Rudolph at right linebacker playing sparingly. Jack and I actually became pretty close. He had played at Georgia Tech and married a girl from Valdosta. Ironically, Jack eventually moved to Valdosta, where he became a defensive coaching legend at my old high school for over thirty years. While in Boston, Jack and his wife kind of looked after me, and they were really the only friends I had.

After living in either Valdosta or Tallahassee all my life, I felt as if I suddenly found myself way up in Boston, as if by surprise. I was "just a good ole country boy from Georgia" who felt totally lost and out of place.

While on full scholarship for five years at Florida State, I had everything done for me, and more; therefore, I barely even knew how to go about finding an apartment to live in. I finally found an apartment rooming with two guys who had been teammates at the same southern school. They eventually didn't want me as a roommate. They didn't like that I played the same newly released album by an up-and-coming country singer all the time on the record player, and my roommates definitely showed their displeasure with my taste in music. The record was *Country Willie—His Own Songs*, the first chart-reaching album by Willie Nelson. Maybe you've heard of him? Shows you what my two roommates knew about music . . .

I did have a girlfriend back in Tallahassee—a real nice FSU sorority girl. We wrote letters back and forth, and telephoned once in a while back when long-distance calling was expensive. Early in the season, I got a letter from her saying she had gone out with another guy, but "it was nothing serious." She said it was just a friendly date to give her something to do. Late in the season, I got another letter from her saying she had gotten married; so much for "it was nothing serious."

I hardly had any friends, no one to hang out with, no more girlfriend back home, and really no one to even talk to, and I was kind of talkative and liked to be social—still do. In Boston, I fit in like a square peg in a round hole. I wasn't happy, and I certainly wasn't playing to my potential.

Approaching mid-November and through the first nine games of the season, and a 1-7-1 record for the Patriots, I was called in to head coach Mike Holovak's office. It was there that Holovak, who was also the team's general manager, said they were letting me go. In all honesty, I didn't mind—not one bit—and still find it humorous to this day that I, a player who couldn't fit in, was released by Boston to make room for a guy who surely had no problem fitting in, rookie linebacker Ed Meixler from Boston University.

I returned home to Valdosta where training camps for the next professional football season, and even graduate school if I decided to go that route, didn't start for an awfully long time. So, to pass the time, you could say, I decided to get back to my country roots. An insurance salesman, Frank Bird, picked me up every morning for the rest of the year and we'd go hunting and fishing.

Mr. Bird took me under his wing (no pun intended), helping a discouraged soul feel, whether playing or coaching, like I still had some football left in me. He always referred to the Good Lord as the "Old Master," and ever since then, so have I.

By that summer, I had been contacted by the Montreal Alouettes, coached by future College Football Hall of Famer Darrell Mudra, of the Canadian Football League (CFL). Out of shape, weighing around 255 pounds, my second time around with professional football, I couldn't even reach the regular season with the team. After playing in only a few exhibition games, I was cut by Mudra, who ironically would eventually be Florida State's head coach in the mid-1970s.

Immediately moving to Atlanta with my older brother, Jack, who was training to be an airline pilot with Delta, I soon got a call from a familiar voice from the past—Perry Moss. Coach Moss had lured me to Florida State back in 1960; six years later, he wanted me to play for him with the Orlando Panthers of the *other* CFL—the Continental Football League.

The CFL had been formed the year before intending to be a top minor league for both the NFL and AFL. From the Wheeling Ironmen to the Toronto Rifles, the league had 10 teams, each with a 36-man roster, and divided into East and West divisions, although every team was more-or-less located on the east coast.

"Coach Moss, I've been cut so many times lately, I'm about to bleed to death," I clearly remember responding to his request. I added that since I couldn't even make it in the Canadian Football League, I was obviously washed up as a player, and was thinking about starting a coaching career. Moss replied that maybe I could coach a little as a part-time assistant under him. Always the salesman, he continued to press, asking me to just come down, hang out, and see if I like it. If anything, he'd take me out a few nights for beers.

Upon reaching Orlando, before I knew it, I was negotiating my own contract with the Orlando Panthers. They would pay me $800 a week during the season, and find me a job for the offseason. And, if I didn't like the job, they'd pay me $400 a week. (Now that I think about it, they never got me a damn job.) Nevertheless, after I got my fat ass in shape, I thoroughly enjoyed my time in Orlando. There, I probably had some of the best times of my life both on and off the field. And, I really liked playing for Coach Moss. He had a smart football mind.

I got to be real close with teammate Glynn Griffing, who had been the starting quarterback of Ole Miss's perfect, 10-0 Sugar Bowl title team of 1962. Although Glynn was married, I'd pick him up about every day and we'd first go shoot pool, play nine holes of golf or so, then grab our shotguns out of the car and go waterhole shoot for doves, and finally go to practice that night. Glynn and I were almost like brothers that football season.

Playing both linebacker and tight end, I had some damn good games for the Panthers. We finished with the best record in the league at 12-2, and Moss was named the

CFL's coach of year in 1966, despite having lost the championship game to the Philadelphia Bulldogs in overtime.

By the end of the season, I realized I was only spinning my wheels: I had bad knees, and I was never getting back into the NFL as a player. If I ever wanted to begin a coaching career, I believed a good idea would be to go back to school and get a master's degree.

I spent the next year, including the 1967 football season, as a graduate assistant at my alma mater, Florida State, and appeared to have a coaching future with the Seminoles—that is, until a family matter got in the way.

My brother Rhett, six years younger than me, received a scholarship to Florida State after being an all-state end at Valdosta High School, where he was the state's Lineman of the Year in 1966. Rhett could catch any damn thing thrown to him. He is still considered one of the greatest receivers in FSU history, and after his induction in 2006, which followed mine from thirteen years earlier, we became the first brothers elected into the FSU Hall of Fame. Rhett actually achieved a better college career than mine, although it got off to a rocky start.

With my brother a true freshman receiver, and me a graduate assistant intending to get my master's in guidance and counseling, Rhett was drilled over the middle by a fellow freshman, defensive back Robert Ashmore, when Rhett was attempting to catch a pass in practice It was nothing dirty, and they were just playing football. It turned out that Rhett was rushed to Tallahassee Memorial Hospital. It was discovered his spleen was ruptured, requiring immediate surgery.

Now, this may not seem like a big deal, but when I was presented the papers to sign, granting the hospital the right to operate on my brother to remove his spleen, it was a rather traumatic experience for me. At the time, I was thinking, here I can barely take care of myself; am I going to have to worry about my brother, as well, while at FSU? I decided right then, the next job offer I received, I was going to take it.

It didn't take long before I got a coaching job offer, and it came from that same familiar voice from my past—Perry Moss. After guiding Orlando to a win in the CFL championship game in 1967, Perry was offered the head coaching job at Marshall University as the Thundering Herd's second choice. Purdue assistant Burnie Miller initially accepted the Marshall job, but wouldn't sign a $15,000-per-year contract.

"I got a job up here for you coaching our secondary, if you want it," Perry said to me over the phone in January 1968. "I'm on my way up!" I declared, and, I truly was. I believe I left that same day, dumping everything I owned, which wasn't much, in the back seat of my 1965 Thunderbird Convertible to hit the road for Marshall University in Huntington, West Virginia. I had never been to West Virginia, or heard of Marshall for that matter, and didn't even know where Huntington was located until getting out a map. I only knew Perry Moss. So, I set out on the 13-hour, 750-mile journey to begin my path to becoming one of the legendary coaches in college football.

Speaking of legendary coaches, Bobby Bowden has often spoken of how he was offered the Marshall head coaching job in 1968. West Virginia's offensive coordinator at the time, Bowden has said he ultimately turned down the job to hold out for an opportunity at a bigger school, which he eventually got in 1970, becoming the head coach of West Virginia. But, just think, as Coach Bowden has said, "I was almost on the plane with Marshall's football team."

In turn, it has been drawn to my attention in recent years that *if*—with a lot of emphasis on the word "if"—Coach Bowden had become head coach of Marshall in 1968, and not Perry Moss, I likely would not have been one of his assistants. Therefore, I would have not only not moved to beautiful Huntington, where I have called home for going on forty-eight years, but most significantly, I would not have been involved in the plane crash—a tragedy that has affected me for most of those forty-eight years.

But, as I said earlier, where I come from, we have a saying for the word "if."

CHAPTER 3
VIOLATIONS AND VICTORIES

When I played college football, players were awarded or forfeited their scholarship in a similar manner as today. For example, if you suffered a career-ending injury, you still kept your scholarship, but if you quit the team, the scholarship was taken away. A lot of players quit when I played college ball—I mean *a lot*. This was especially the case at an up-and-coming program like Florida State, where often the toughness of a player was as important to the coaching staff as his athleticism.

From my room at FSU's Smith Hall, I can still hear it today, echoing throughout the dorm: "Forget this stuff!" although usually a different f-word and s-word were used, or "I don't have to take this stuff!" would be yelled night after night, accompanied by a slamming door, and another player walking out of the dorm, and out of the program.

If a scholarship player didn't appear tough enough, or good enough, the coaches would normally attempt to run him off if he didn't first quit on his own. During my first couple of years at FSU, what I lacked in on-field ability, I tried to more than make up for with toughness. Toughness was displayed usually through fighting—literally—at practice. The idea was the coaches were going to play the toughest guy at the position; therefore, I had to show I was the toughest by fighting for that position.

I had made up my mind that I was *not* going to be run out of the program. I had no other choice. Where was I going to go—back home to Valdosta as a quitter to face my daddy? So, I'd fight anyone at practice just to show everyone how tough I was, and it didn't matter to me at first if I won or not. I feel kind of bad and embarrassed about it today, but I probably started more fights on the Florida State practice field than anyone during my time. There were a lot of good athletes at the end position, my position, fighting for playing time.

Defensive line coach Dick Flowers, who had played at Alabama along with our athletic director, Vaughn Mancha, was highly respected, but could also be the chief instigator. I might go over to Coach Flowers's house during the day, where we would shoot pool, and he'd give me a sandwich and a Coke. But, later that afternoon/evening during practice, he would be firing me up to fight. Coach Flowers would get me so charged up, I'd then go haul off and hit an upperclassman in the damn nose. Flowers appeared to love it, and he made me think as a thin, unaccomplished, true freshman-turned-redshirt from 1960–1961 that maybe one of these days I *can* play!

By the time I was a sophomore, weighing between 215 and 220 pounds, I *was* playing. No longer was there any reason for me to start fights and no one seemed to want to fight me.

As soon as I got to Marshall University in January 1968, the subject of toughness immediately came up. Overall, the Thundering Herd players returning from the 1967 season needed more of it, and the sooner the better. The practice sessions the returners had experienced under the previous regime were "a piece of cake," as it was described to me. This probably was good reason why the program had severely slipped from three consecutive non-losing seasons from 1963 through 1965 to a 2-8 record in 1966 followed by a winless 0-10 mark.

With Perry Moss's arrival, spring practice at Marshall was suddenly transformed from a "piece of cake" to being very tough, with the idea that it would get a little easier as the year wore on and as the players began to develop. Very tough is all that Perry, me, and most of the other assistants knew. This is how it was going to be at Marshall if the program had any hope of developing into a contender in our conference, the then-seven-member MAC (Mid-American Conference). Clearly, we wanted to see who could play football—and who couldn't.

I've since heard from players who went through the spring of 1968 that water was given to them at practice only as a treat. This is actually more or less accurate. It's also been said there was always an ambulance present at practice in clear view for "psychological" reasons.

When I played at Florida State, the idea was to get in shape during the spring, and to help one do so, there were no water breaks during practice. We had the same philosophy upon arriving at Marshall. We all now realize this was quite dangerous, but at the same time, it was just a reality. As a player, I once lost 16 pounds during a single practice. Before there were sports drinks, and we had salt pills taped to our hip pads to take during practice to replenish sodium. Eventually, we got a little smarter when our team physician, Dr. Bob Johnson, and head trainer, Don Fauls, created "Seminole Firewater," a good-tasting lime drink containing sugar and salt for a readily digestible carbohydrate to drink following practice.

A side note, if you look it up, you'll find some debate on which came first—our Seminole Firewater or the University of Florida's Gatorade—and if the makers of Gatorade actually copied Florida State's sports-drink formula. This is all I know: I was drinking Seminole Firewater while at Florida State, which was before Florida introduced its Gatorade in 1965. From what I remember, Seminole Firewater tasted a lot like today's Gatorade. I'm just saying . . .

As far as an ambulance being present during practice, I only recall that occurring one time. It's a kind of funny story that really isn't funny at all. As a relatively young assistant coaching staff not too far removed from our playing days, we decided that if need be during practice, whether to help toughen up the players, or to fill in for the missing ones that had quit, we should participate during some of their drills. This was the case for all of the assistants except one in particular who wasn't very nimble on his feet and therefore was advised to only coach from the sideline. During one particular practice though, this coach didn't take our advice and got caught up in a scrum of players. The next thing I knew, he was hollering under a pile of bodies that his leg hurt. I ran over to him, lifted his left leg, and holy crap! It was awful: it was so badly broken it looked as if his ankle and foot were literally dangling from his leg attached only by his sock! "Hold on, you've broken your leg," I told the coach as he rolled around in pain while I tried to hold him down. "Someone call a damn ambulance!"

These tough practices, of course, helped clarify which existing players would be able to handle the current system. And, which players would not, like one whose father actually demanded from the university that I be fired for being "abusive" to his son . . . for making the player run wind sprints, of all things. I believe Perry soon realized he might not be able to completely turn around the Marshall program with the players already at hand, but would have to intensely recruit, bringing in his own players to build a winner.

Recruiting high school players to come to Marshall could be an uphill battle—literally. Our stadium at the time, grass-surfaced Fairfield Stadium, which we shared with a couple of high schools, was built on an old garbage dump, where one end slightly sloped up from the end zone to around the 35-yard line because the dirt underneath had become unstable over time. With an inadequate stadium, and sub-par facilities overall, coupled with little money coming in to the program, we didn't have a whole lot of ammunition with which to recruit. So, it was decided we had to think outside the box, so to speak, to lure recruits.

Prior to 1968, whether it was entirely accurate or not, Marshall's football team was characterized as being made up of players from West Virginia that West Virginia University didn't want, boys from Ohio that no one in the Big Ten wanted, and junior college players no one had heard of. However, by the winter of my first year at Marshall, the program benefitted from some extra funds via fundraising by boosters belonging to Marshall's Big Green Club. With the additional funding, we expanded the recruiting into faraway states like Texas and New Jersey, as well as Alabama and Florida—my primary recruiting ground. Hundreds of letters were sent all over the country, asking players to come try out at Marshall for a good chance at getting a football scholarship. Honestly, at the time, I had no idea we were committing NCAA violations by requesting tryouts.

I can still see the scene in my mind. There were at least 100, maybe as many as 150, freshman recruits who had traveled to little Marshall—a university ranking toward the bottom of state-funded schools in West Virginia, featuring a football program that was seemingly not far off from becoming defunct—to try out for the Thundering Herd football team.

We could give full scholarships to only thirty-five recruits. Those were reserved for the likes of quarterback Ted Shoebridge from New Jersey, one of the most highly touted signal callers coming out of high school; lineman Ron Mikolajczyk, also from New Jersey, who at only seventeen years old was already "a man" at six-foot-four and 250 pounds (which was absolutely *huge* back in 1968, especially for Marshall); Dennis Blevins from Bluefield, West Virginia, who, besides being an all-state basketball player and a standout in track, was a wide receiver who could flat-out fly; and defensive back Larry Sanders from Tuscaloosa, Alabama. Alabama's head coach, Paul "Bear" Bryant, had turned me on to Sanders by calling our football office and explaining there was a bright, strong, rugged kid at Druid High School, named Sanders, who we should give a scholarship to because he was eventually going to play in the pros. I'll never forget when I was just about to head down to Tuscaloosa to take a look at Larry when a school administrator stopped me to ask about the "black boy" from Alabama I was going to sign.

"Well, you don't want to sign too many blacks from down there!" the administrator declared. I responded by saying I was only trying to recruit the best players to put on the field to represent Marshall. As long as they were good citizens, tough, and could play football, I didn't care what color they were. Thus, Sanders became a member of the team.

If a player did well enough in tryouts but wasn't given one of the thirty-five scholarships, we had them fill out financial aid forms and instructed them to go to a bank in downtown Huntington. Although coaches obviously cannot arrange for an athlete to receive an athletic loan, the bank was alerted which recruits would qualify for a federally insured student loan. And, since the Educational Opportunity Act to help the poor finance college educations had recently been implemented, any impoverished

African American player we sent to the bank essentially received a full scholarship, as well, in the form of a loan. For those who didn't qualify, they could also receive financial aid through the bank in the form of a student loan, but it would be a loan they'd eventually have to pay back.

Now, I've always claimed I was only following orders regarding the whole bank-loan ordeal, which is true. But, in all honesty, I really didn't stop and ask myself if what we were doing was against the rules. We all just did what we were told. However, if I had stopped for a moment, I probably would have figured we were committing violations. From the coaches down to the trainers, we *all* probably would have decided it was against the rules. Of course, offensive line coach Jim "Shorty" Moss (no relation to Perry), a Huntington native who had been a standout at West Virginia when I was at Florida State, perhaps had the highest set of morals of anyone I've ever known. And, if he even had the slightest inkling we were committing NCAA violations, my guess is that he wouldn't have taken part.

In the end, we signed over fifty recruits to the 1968 Little Herd freshman team, including other highly touted newcomers like halfback Art Harris from New Jersey; six-foot-five lineman Jim Sly from Iaeger, West Virginia; Stacy Poullard, who was considered one of the fastest high school running backs in the entire country, from Louisiana; and hard-hitting defensive back Nate Ruffin from Quincy, Florida, who I'd personally recruited.

These bright prospects were unfortunately only eligible to play on what was seemingly going to be an excellent freshman squad. On the contrary, the varsity Thundering Herd was the preseason pick to end up exactly where it had finished the previous two seasons (dead last in the MAC). The coaching staff's first game at Marshall—a matchup against Morehead State—would actually mark a memorable moment, as it was the program's only non-loss during a losing stretch which wound up lasting almost three entire years. Trailing Morehead State 7-0 in the second quarter, quarterback Don Swisher threw a short scoring pass to Charlie Jones to tie the game. The score held, ending our opener with a 7-7 draw. Actually, we were really fortunate we didn't lose, as Morehead State totally outplayed us, rushing for over 200 yards and forcing us to commit five turnovers. But, to our advantage, they missed three field goals, including two chip shots.

After getting routed by Ohio and Toledo, making our record 0-2-1, it was made clear that our focus as a staff should include coaching the freshmen players, as well. Even Perry started concentrating on the Little Herd, coaching them some during practice, though they couldn't play in varsity games. Prohibited by the NCAA to play varsity ball because they were freshmen, the Little Herd routinely defeated the older Thundering Herd in scrimmages.

On a Thursday in early October, practice was cut early so we could make the two-hour trip west to Lexington, Kentucky, to see the Little Herd play. They were coached by Pete Kondos and faced the University of Kentucky frosh in their season opener. Before the game in the press box, Kentucky's head varsity coach, Charley Bradshaw, approached Perry and I and boasted, "These are the finest freshmen athletes Kentucky football has ever had in one year!" Granted, Coach Bradshaw was apparently very optimistic. A few weeks later, he claimed his 2-3 varsity Wildcats were "the best 2-3 football team in America" just before they were soundly defeated by their opponent. Nevertheless, the fact Kentucky's freshman team featured future Southeastern Conference players, whereas the Little Herd players were destined to be members of the lowly Marshall varsity, was reason enough to think if the Dunkel Index gave out forecasts for freshman games, a Marshall miraculous defeat over Kentucky would surely rank right up there with Florida State's victory over Kentucky in 1964 as one of the biggest upsets in college football history.

What was called a "domination" over "the highly-touted Kentucky freshmen," the Little Herd blew the Wildcats' finest freshmen athletes out of their own damn stadium with a 27-16 victory. Shoebridge guided Marshall to over 400 yards of total offense. In comparison, the Thundering Herd the previous season had averaged less than 150 total yards per game (yes, 150, that's not a misprint). Both Kondos and Perry were absolutely thrilled, commenting to the media afterward, "[The Little Herd] proved to me that they liked to hit." But, most importantly, they proved that Marshall football's misfortunes would likely soon be history, starting the very next season when the freshmen phenoms would be sophomores on the varsity squad. As for me, I remember being pretty excited as well. However, I couldn't help but think that although defeating Kentucky seemed like a historic victory, the improbable win would soon put the freshman team under a microscope, and thus the program's conceivably questionable recruiting practices could come back to bite us in the ass.

Losing games by an average margin of more than 25 points, the varsity squad finished winless in 1968 at 0-9-1, extending Marshall's non-winning streak to 21 games. On the contrary, the freshman team followed the victory at Kentucky with wins over Dayton, Xavier, and Ohio—all on the road. They finished with a home victory over West Virginia Tech for a perfect 5-0 season.

Essentially having to concentrate on two different football teams, it's a wonder any of the coaches had time for a social life. But, as I've indicated, I liked to be social back then, so something had to give.

I was fortunate to become close with the team physician, Pete Proctor, soon after I got to Marshall. He introduced me to another doctor, Ray Hagley, and the pair of physicians helped me, a twenty-six-year-old bachelor with little time to do anything unrelated to football, get more acquainted with Huntington and its people. I got to know a number of community leaders and became familiar with many football boosters of the Big Green Club. Early on, Pete even got me a date with a local girl, Carole. She and I became serious rather quickly and married in December, or less than a year after my move to Huntington. Our honeymoon in Atlanta included watching Florida State play

LSU in the Peach Bowl, and I spent a lot of the remaining time recruiting. After only two or three days, I had to return to Huntington to get back to recruiting. The life of a college football coach . . .

During that winter, no longer in need of a nationwide letter-writing campaign or bank loans to help in recruiting, we put together another wide-ranging class. From Texas, we lured all-district lineman Ed Carter and "do-everything" Bobby Joe Hill, a five-foot-ten, 160-pound speedster, who could play quarterback, running back, receiver, or even on the defensive side of the ball. From nearby, we signed two all-state linemen: Mike Blake from Huntington and Jack Crabtree from Virginia. Finally, we landed a real rarity in college football for back then: a soccer-style, long-distant placekicker, Marcelo Lajterman, who had been a high school teammate of Shoebridge's in Lyndhurst, New Jersey. Marcelo seemed to be as reliable as Les Murdock had been five years before at Florida State. Still, just as we were shoring up our incoming class, the process used to recruit the class the year before indeed came back to bite us.

It's been said that a recruit from 1968, who had supposedly been receiving cash payments, stopped going to practice, and in turn, Marshall's athletic department stopped his payments. The recruit allegedly became disgruntled, informed a relative who had ties with another MAC school of his dilemma, and the relative informed the conference of the ordeal. As indicated, I was fully aware of the massive tryout we had. Hell, I tried out a lot of those guys myself and knew about the loans through the bank. However, I was totally unaware of any cash payments given to players. I was oblivious we did anything seriously wrong until Marshall's new president, Dr. Roland Nelson, appointed a committee in February 1969 to investigate if any violations were committed by the school's athletic programs, particularly the football team.

In May, the committee disclosed we had committed 144 recruiting infractions. Nelson reported these findings to the MAC, who launched its own investigation in June. Soon afterward, Marshall decided to launch a separate investigation, wherein President Nelson appointed a "Three-Man Committee" to respond to questions from the MAC Council of Presidents.

A spokesman for President Nelson held a press conference, whereupon it appeared charges would be brought against only those who had organized the wrongdoings. I was in the clear, or so I thought. I soon received a letter indicating I was to appear before the Three-Man Committee. The letter questioned my character, indicating I had been "personally charged," although no specific charges were mentioned. I was asked to defend myself in front of the committee. I also was extended the opportunity to have witnesses or advisors speak on my behalf.

I was scared shitless! I was a naive, twenty-six-year-old asked to appear before a committee for the first time in my life, and had no idea of with what I had even been charged. As for me having advisors or witnesses, for what? Who would I even ask to speak on my behalf?

Although the spokesman would inform me and the others "charged" that the committee was not working against us, but simply gathering information to present to the MAC, I sought out a lawyer who helped me prepare a statement to read.

Concerned, confused, scared for my job, and uncertain regarding my future as a coach at *any* school, I stood in front of the committee, where I was first assured that any information I provided would go no further than President Nelson. It was indicated that the president only needed the information to assist him in responding to the questions posed by the conference's council of presidents. I then began to read my prepared statement when, less than fifteen seconds into it, all three committee members began laughing, almost howling. One member stopped his laughing long enough to say something on the order that "this isn't *that* kind of hearing." "This is very informal; you're not being charged with anything," and I was taking things too seriously and didn't need to read any kind of statement. As he spoke, I recognized one of the other two members, a former assistant football coach at Marshall from about a decade before, with whom I was very familiar. Ironically, this particular committee member was widely known when he coached to allegedly paying Thundering Herd players (and assuredly not from his own pocket) $15 for beating a conference opponent, $10 for defeating a non-conference foe, and $4 for losing but playing a good game. And, here he would soon be questioning me for only doing what I was told to do.

After everyone was questioned by the committee, Nelson revealed our answers in July to the MAC Council of Presidents, who kicked us out of the conference "indefinitely." The NCAA later placed the program on probation for a year.

Following the conference's ruling, Nelson presented a report from the committee to Marshall's University Council and the Athletic Committee, asking for their recommendations. So much for being assured that any information I provided would go no further than President Nelson.

In late July, the joint committee asked three Marshall head coaches, including Perry and head freshman coach Kondos, who also served as recruiting coordinator, to present their stance on the alleged infractions. In the end, or less than a month prior to our 1969 season opener, Kondos was fired, Perry was reassigned to a non-coaching position in the athletic department, and by then, our athletic director, Edgar Barrett, had resigned. It wasn't a pretty time.

As soon as we were put on probation followed by Perry's reassignment, Marshall players started dropping like flies. Most of them left because they didn't want to play for a program on probation, or they had signed to play under Perry and if he was no longer part of the team, neither were they. In addition, about a dozen failed to earn a legitimate scholarship after first being granted a governmental loan.

As far as the coaching staff, Ken Cooper, the defensive coordinator in 1968, left in the offseason when Perry was still head coach. I was promoted to defensive coordinator and Rick Tolley, a tough son-of-a-gun, was hired from Wake Forest to coach our defensive line.

Rick had played at Virginia Tech and in 1965 became the first full-time coach to assist the acclaimed Hank Norton of Ferrum Junior College. Ferrum, Virginia, located about 250 miles southeast of Huntington, won four junior college national championships under Norton, including titles in 1965 and 1968. I've always said if a boy played football at Ferrum back then, they must've been pretty damn good, but more so, tough. Ferrum featured few superstar-like players, but by God, it seemed they all could lay a lick on an opposing player. In my first three seasons coaching at Marshall, I'm sure we had at least a half-dozen former Ferrum players annually on our roster, most of whom were offensive and defensive linemen, or linebackers, and about all were heavy hitters.

I got to know Rick real well soon after he came to Marshall when he and Coach Norton took a trip with me to Valdosta to do some fishing. Rick was from Mullens, West Virginia—coal country—and grew up tough. However, besides having a hard demeanor, he was genuinely a really good guy—a hell of a man. He would soon demonstrate he was also a hell of a coach.

Perry's reassignment meant we had no head coach with only a couple of days remaining before we opened fall camp. Acting quickly, President Nelson appointed twenty-nine-year-old Rick Tolley—a logical choice—for the vacant position on an interim basis. By doing so, Rick became one of the youngest head football coaches in all of college football. And, if the Thundering Herd players thought practices were tough under Perry, they hadn't experienced anything yet!

In early September, our coaching staff was finalized with the hiring of a new assistant, Ken O'Rourke. Months before, I evidently didn't heed the advice of the Marshall administrator who recommended the year prior I not sign too many black players "from down there." In year two, we signed *four* players from Druid High in Tuscaloosa. Apparently, their signings helped lure O'Rourke, a black assistant coach at Druid, who replaced Kondos as Marshall's new freshman coach. However, on the day we gained a coach, we lost two more players—both defensive backs, including a starter—dropping our team total to only forty-one players, or less than half the number on our roster in the spring.

Getting ready for the season during a fall camp described as "like a Marine boot camp," the team was relieved when a couple of players who had left the program decided to return—formerly star freshmen with lofty expectations as members of Marshall's varsity as sophomores—quarterback Ted Shoebridge and lineman Ron Mikolajczyk.

Whereas almost forty Marshall players have played in the NFL the last fifteen years, just one reached the professional level in about a fifteen-year period from the late 1960s to the early 1980s—Mikolajczyk. Mikolajczyk played on the '68 freshman team and then, after returning from quitting, was a member of the varsity for only a couple of practices until quitting again, leaving for the University of Tampa.

Fortunately for us, Shoebridge stayed, while we also gained another player who had previously left—a player I might have been a little partial to—offensive lineman David DeBord. DeBord, a small, but strong and agile offensive lineman, had attended Marion Institute Junior College in Alabama after I had known him as a boy. The son of Florida State's long-time equipment manager, Frank DeBord, David had grown up in the Tallahassee area. Looking to play football after junior college, he had a hard time considering any other school besides Marshall and I recruited and eventually signed him.

Despite having some really good talent at most positions, especially Shoebridge at quarterback, we had little depth, and it showed as we routinely seemed to be within striking distance of our opponent at halftime, if not leading the game, but would crumble in the second half. Heading into the month of November, we were in a predicament that we had grown accustomed to: *winless*, at 0-6.

Undefeated the season before, the Little Herd wasn't doing much better. Playing only three games for the season, the freshman team lost all of them. However, they nearly won at Kentucky *again*, losing 32-31. From that team, enough can't be said about the play of the newcomers we signed from Druid High. Of the four, one would quit, but it became evident that tight end Freddy Wilson and defensive tackle Robert VanHorn were going to be really good varsity players. And then, there was Joe Hood, who I still say is the best running back I've ever seen. At six-foot-one, 200 pounds, Joe could have played for any big-time program in the South, if he hadn't been black. In the late 1960s, most southern programs were either still not signing black players, or were going about it gingerly. On that year's freshman squad, Joe overwhelmingly was the team leader in rushing, receiving, kickoff returns, and punt returns. He was so talented, they also even let him pass the ball out of the backfield seven or eight times per game. Besides Joe, the freshman placekicker, Lajterman, was said to eventually have the best chance at a professional football career. Making seven of his 10 placekicks in the three losses, he was already getting some attention from pro scouts.

Worse than being winless on the season, the varsity was just one loss away from tying the major college record shared by Virginia and Kansas State for the longest non-winning streak at 28 straight games. But, I believe it was this streak, and the strong desire to avoid extending it and joining the two disgraced schools, that generated a school spirit like few I've experienced.

Next on the schedule was the Homecoming game against Bowling Green. Based on the preparation by Marshall students, one would have thought we were riding a 27-game non-losing streak instead of the opposite. It was dubbed "Stop the Streak Week," and soon, countless "Stop the Streak" banners, signs, and stickers became affixed to dormitories, buildings, and automobiles. It was tremendous support for what seemed most likely to be a near-hopeless cause.

Under second-year head coach and future West Virginia coaching great Don Nehlen, Bowling Green came to Huntington having suffered just one loss in the MAC. It was believed the Thundering Herd was just one more step—and a small one at that—on the Falcons' path to the Tangerine Bowl, which began a conference tie-in with the MAC champion the year before. I remember seeing in the newspaper a couple days before the game a prediction from the Harmon Forecast, predicting a 31-to-*nothing* victory for Bowling Green.

After the Falcons took an early 6-0 lead, Shoebridge connected on two long touchdown passes to Dickie Carter and Jack Repasy, respectively. We led 14-6 at halftime; however, Marshall had been in similar positions before until faltering down the stretch. In the fourth quarter, our offense mounted another drive. We had the ball on the one-foot line, facing fourth down and goal, and junior Kevin Gilmore got the call. Gilmore, another New Jersey boy, was probably the most versatile player on that team. He was a good defensive back, returned kickoffs and punts, and, of course, could run the ball out of the backfield, as well. Gilmore blasted into the end zone for a touchdown, giving us a comfortable 21-6 advantage, but the game was far from over.

Bowling Green's quarterback, Vern Wireman, threw all over us that day for about 300 yards, and in the process made me look pretty damn sorry as a defensive coordinator. He took the Falcons right down the field for a touchdown and a two-point conversion. Trailing 21-14, Bowling

Green had the ball around our 40-yard line. Wireman threw a long pass near our goal line, but there for an interception was the Thundering Herd player who would have never been at Marshall in the first place if it wasn't for a phone call from "Bear" Bryant—Larry Sanders.

Backed up near our own goal line, we gave Bowling Green an intentional safety before finally prevailing, 21-16. With the improbable resulting, the streak had been stopped—finally! A huge celebration followed, both on the field by swarming fans, and later in Huntington. You would have thought we won a national championship.

As far as enduring and unfortunately being part of such an embarrassing streak, I'd say every player and coach—every one of us—was confident it was only a matter of time (and not much time) until it ended. There may have been only a few of us that honestly believed it would end against heavily-favored Bowling Green; however, what was left of that 1969 team—after all the guys who didn't want to be at Marshall took off—was a talented and tough group of guys. And, it's been my experience that if a talented and tough program is losing, it doesn't lose for long. And, sooner or later, the only streaks it experiences are of the winning kind.

After the win over Bowling Green, a funny thing happened: two more victories in a row. First, we defeated Kent State 31-20 on the road. This was Marshall's first away-game win since early in the 1965 season. Next we beat East Carolina by a staggering 38-7 score—the Thundering Herd's biggest margin of victory in a single game in more than fourteen years. The defense was spectacular against the Pirates, allowing only about 200 total yards and a single touchdown. Following the win, I was given an ultimate honor when the team presented me with the game ball, my third game ball at that time. I was presented with my first as a player at Florida State and my second while playing for the Orlando Panthers.

With a 3-6 record and our season finale against Ohio University just days away, almost thirty players suddenly signed a petition to have Perry reinstated as head coach, to be given to the governor of West Virginia, Arch Moore. Their argument was the same as the one many had given regarding why they had left the program just months before: they had signed to play under Moss and if he wasn't going to be part of the team, neither were they.

I'm not sure if the petition became a distraction for the Thundering Herd, but I do know what was known as a "first-half team" suddenly wasn't against Ohio in Huntington. Trailing 24-7 at halftime, we finally decided to wake up in the second half. Behind Shoebridge, who broke a number of Marshall game and season records against the Bobcats—including most yards passing in a game (312)—we outscored Ohio 28-7 to take a late lead, 35-31. However, the Bobcats drove down the field in the final minute and scored on a one-yard plunge with just five seconds remaining to win.

After Ohio's winning touchdown, some enraged fans, presumably upset at the officials for the Bobcats' victory, jumped from the stands and went after a couple of the officials. The scene was a mess: fans assaulting officials and police trying to restore order, while we were still getting over having just lost a heartbreaking game in the final seconds! Soon, even some people from the university, including a coach or two, had to step in to calm things down. I remember spotting my buddy Frank, my replacement as secondary coach, and thinking, if I'm forced to fight my way out of here, good thing he's on my side.

Just like the players had a nickname for Coach Tolley because of his toughness—"Dog Man" or "Hard Rock"—they also had one for Frank Loria—"Little Rock"— for the very same reason. Small, but chiseled in stature, Frank played in the same defensive backfield with coaching great Frank Beamer at Virginia Tech during the mid-1960s. A consensus All-American in 1967, Frank eventually had his number retired by the school. When I first met Frank in 1969, who was still in his early twenties, I somewhat prejudged him as a little showoff All-American, who could no longer hot-dog it as a player, so he was going to try to do so as a coach. However, it didn't take long for me to realize I had made a very poor judgment.

Frank was a man's man, and as sound a man as I've ever met in every way. Occasionally, at night after we had studied film of the upcoming opponent or some high school prospects, Frank would proudly put on film of him playing for Virginia Tech. But, the film wasn't of him excelling at what got his No. 10 retired or what put him in the College Football Hall of Fame—intercepting passes and returning punts—but when his coaches, for goal-line situations, would move him from defensive back to middle linebacker—all five-foot-nine, 175 pounds of him. Frank was as good a goal-line middle linebacker as I've ever seen at any level. To make a tackle, he always approached the ball-carrier so that the top of his helmet would spear the opposing player right up under the chin—*wham!* What Frank gave away in size, he more than made up with heart.

There's a football saying that "you play the way you practice." After watching film of Frank at Virginia Tech, and how he conducted himself as a coach at Marshall, he must have lived by the adage, "you coach the way you played"—all toughness, all heart. Prominently featuring "Hard Rock" and "Little Rock," the entire Marshall coaching staff characterized toughness, whereas the team in 1969 had finally played the way it practiced—*tough*—and it had paid off in the end. Returning seven starters on offense and nine starters on defense, the 1970 Thundering Herd looked to finally put Marshall football on the map.

CHAPTER 4
100 PERCENT, BIG LEAGUE

Because of my personal experience with one of my fellow coaches at Marshall, kicking coach Deke Brackett, I decided back then that a rule of thumb for younger people like myself at the time should be to cultivate the friendship of old men. Old men generally give good advice. They have experienced a lot in their lifetimes, and young people can learn a great deal from them.

Entering the 1970 season, Deke was in his late fifties. This seemed old to the rest of a coaching staff composed of men in their twenties and thirties, and he certainly had experienced a lot. After playing quarterback at the University of Tennessee in the early 1930s, Deke was a college assistant coach for roughly thirty consecutive years, which included stops at Tennessee, Arkansas, and UCLA. He later coached under Perry Moss with the Orlando Panthers in 1967, and then followed him to Marshall the next year.

Besides giving great advice and being an experienced football coach, Deke might have had the most unique personality of any coach in the history of college football. He loved poetry, so much so that he had Rudyard Kipling's *The Mary Gloster* memorized—word for word, more than 2,300 of them. Deke was full of expressions, like "100 percent, big league," a phrase he would always use to give someone or something the ultimate compliment. And he seemed to have a story for every occasion.

Deke's favorite story, one I heard him share so many times in the three years I coached with him that I eventually had it memorized, was a story he swore was true. He had heard it while he was coaching at Arkansas in the late 1940s about when the State Congress was going to vote on whether to change the state's name from "Arkansas" to "Ar-kansas."

I can still see Deke in my mind now, explaining how changing the state's name was once a sure thing—an anticipated landslide vote for "Ar-kansas." Just before the vote, the Speaker of the House was interrupted by a booming voice in the back of the room belonging to Senator Hiram Johnson. Johnson was from Johnson County, or "a place so dang tough, a man dare not hang his ass from a second-story window to take a decent shit, for fear of getting his ass shot with bird shot," according to Deke, quoting Johnson.

As the story goes, Senator Johnson began explaining how tough someone had to be from Johnson County, Arkansas, beginning at a young age and counting up:

> *. . . where at the age of fourteen, I stood all day at the hitching post thinking I was hitched. Where at the age of fifteen, I could piss halfway across the Red River. . .*

"Out of order! Out of order!" interrupted the Speaker. Johnson responded, "You're dang right it was out of order, or I'd have pissed all the damn way across!"

Johnson continued by saying he had traveled all over the United States, and nowhere was it more beautiful than the state of Arkansas. He declared some terrible things could be allowed to impair certain meaningful images of America; however . . .

> *Change the name of Arkansas to Ar-kansas? Not "no," but "hell no!" Not until the great Mississippi, the father of all waters, floats with horse turds as big as the Rock of Gibraltar!*

JOHNSON WAS FINISHED. THE Speaker took the vote, and as expected, it was indeed a landslide; however, not for "Ar-kansas," but an easy victory for keeping the state's name of "Arkansas."

I loved Deke Brackett—still do.

Deke, Frank Loria, and I generally rode to practice together, and entering the spring of 1970, we could all feel a different vibe surrounding the program than what had lingered during previous springs. I'm sure every coach and player could tell a difference. For once, we were no longer riding a long non-winning streak, but had actually won three of our previous four games, with the loss against Ohio in Huntington being a game we undoubtedly should have won.

Simply put, things had changed, and for the better—that is, *mostly* for the better.

Upon arriving at the first spring practice in early April of 1970, I noticed Roger Childers, a sophomore, filling a role he didn't prefer and was unaccustomed to as a team manager. However, "100 percenter"—that's what I called Roger because that's what he gave every second he was on the football field—would do absolutely anything just to be a part of the Marshall football program.

In my first summer at Marshall in 1968, while players were quitting because they thought the practices were too tough, Childers showed an eagerness and drive like no other. After making the team as a freshman walk-on, Roger earned a starting linebacker spot entering the following season as only a sophomore and still without a scholarship. To show the diversity of that team, Roger was the only defensive starter from the state of West Virginia—St. Albans, West Virginia, to be exact—less than an hour east of Huntington. Weighing only about 175 pounds, Roger was also one of just two starting linebackers we had in the uncommon 6-2-3 defensive formation Marshall used in '69. We basically had no choice but to use the 6-2-3 because of our inexperience and lack of depth.

In winning three of our final four games, Roger spearheaded our defense down the stretch. In a game at Kent State and on scholarship by that time, he intercepted two passes and blocked a punt, our only blocked punt the entire season. Against East Carolina, Roger picked off another pass. He ended the season with the second-most interceptions on the team with four. Finally in the loss against Ohio, he wanted to win so badly that when the Bobcat ball carrier crossed our goal line for the game-winning touchdown on the final play, Roger was overcome with frustration and emotion and moved to tears.

Of course, it was a blow to hear during the 1970 off-season that a player I wished I had eleven of starting on defense wasn't able to play that season, nor probably ever. In February, Roger had to undergo a six-hour surgery to remove a brain tumor. The tumor was removed, but hearing was lost in his right ear, the right side of his face was completely paralyzed, and he was facing an additional surgery. Although his return to playing football seemed rather unlikely, Roger talked about hoping to redshirt in 1970, so he wouldn't waste a year. And, I'll never forget once when he was talking about losing the ability to hear in his right ear, he added something on the order of "I still have my left one."

On the football field in 1969, Roger Childers was tireless, full of confidence, in better shape than the next guy, and as tough as they come. On the sideline entering the 1970 season, he was still giving 100 percent—only this time, as a team manager.

Roger said entering the season, "Things are looking up at Marshall. And, I want to be part of it, and I will be again." It's a statement I still think of whenever I don't feel like giving something my all.

Despite the petition signed by the twenty-five to thirty Marshall players prior to the final game of the 1969 season to have Perry reinstated the following year as head coach (a position he went as far as applying for), Rick Tolley was promoted from acting to permanent head coach soon after the season ended. After Rick's promotion, superstar quarterback Ted Shoebridge was supposedly questioning for the second time whether to return to Marshall. Rick was asked about Shoebridge possibly not returning, and confidently stated to the press, "I know Ted will be back." He then declared we were expecting *all* the players back, without question—most of which had wanted Perry, not Rick, as their head coach. Ending with some humor, Rick then said he expected all the players from the year before back, that is, except the graduating seniors. It was the same display of assuredness and confidence Rick seemed to always possess. Similarly, when we were only able to suit up about thirty-five players for most of the 1969 season and recognized the remote possibility of a healthy starting eleven on offense or defense being fielded, Rick never panicked. "At least, not until we're down to ten players," he once said.

In 1970, the cupboard wasn't as bare, but it was far from full. We had to switch some players around to accommodate the depth at certain positions. Most notably, we were short on linebackers but had plenty of running backs. So, Willie Bluford was moved from fullback and instantly became Roger's replacement as a starting linebacker.

Our only player from South Carolina, Willie originally signed out of high school with Livingstone College—a small, historically black school in North Carolina. The next thing I knew, within a week of Willie's signing, Perry had somehow talked him into spurning Livingstone and signing with Marshall (at a time when a player signing to attend a school bounded the school to the player, but not necessarily the player to the school).

A bruising fullback who could catch the ball out of the backfield as well, Willie was one of the stars on the '68 undefeated freshman team. After backing up Dickie Carter at fullback on the varsity the next season, Willie physically seemed ideal to take over Roger's linebacker spot, while having the same I-don't-care-where-I-play-just-so-I-play attitude. Once he was at the position in the spring, we realized we had made a good decision. Willie was naturally a hard hitter—a real headhunter.

We had talented players, like Willie, at most starting positions, and again, Marshall had recruited well. We actually signed a defensive lineman, Greg Finn, nicknamed "Huck," out of a junior college in Nebraska. He was considered maybe the best junior college player in the country. Major programs from all over the country wanted him, including "Bear" Bryant's Alabama. Finn initially signed with Alabama, but he would ultimately turn his back on the Bear and sign with Marshall.

Still, of our thirty signees that year, twenty-five were true freshmen and ineligible to play varsity, leaving the Thundering Herd with talented starters, and seemingly a bright future, but very little depth for the 1970 season.

The team roster wasn't the only thing undergoing a major transformation. Put to rest was old "downhill lie," or what Marshall players called the sloping grass surface of Fairfield Stadium. When it was still considered cutting-edge, before it seemed every pro and college team started installing it during the 1970s and 1980s, AstroTurf replaced Fairfield's grass. In addition, new dressing rooms were constructed, and the stadium added several thousand new seats, bringing Fairfield's capacity to roughly a dozen thousand or so.

Well, I guess if you get a new field, you have to get a new mascot to roam around on it, so that's what was done. Courtney Proctor, the wife of my doctor friend, Pete Proctor, thought the football team should have a real live buffalo mascot instead of just a costumed version. Pete bought a buffalo in Indiana and drove it to the Proctorville Fairgrounds in Ohio, located about ten miles from Huntington. Pete got in touch with me one day and said he was having a hard time handling Marco, the new live buffalo, and asked if I could help out. We drove over to the fairgrounds and Pete showed me the buffalo. It was just a young calf at that point, and by appearances, looked very manageable. Now, I was a big guy back then, built about the same as when I had played pro ball a few years before. Regardless, when I grabbed the calf by what horns he had, Marco went absolutely mad, tossing me around like a child. Needless to say, I couldn't handle him either.

By the start of the season, Marco had grown a little and had his own personalized trailer for transportation. A few years before, Colorado had started the tradition of running its live buffalo, Ralphie, on the field. Marco's handlers thought their buffalo could do the same, but I guess no one told them that Ralphie was trained to run. On the contrary, Marco wasn't trained—far from it. Regardless, it would take a little while before it was decided that having a live, untrained buffalo probably wasn't the thing to do.

For the 1970 season opener against Morehead State at the "new" Fairfield Stadium, another drastic change had occurred: we were actually favored entering a ballgame. Despite officially no longer belonging to the MAC because of the recruiting violations, we still got the season started in style when defensive end Dave Griffith nailed the returner on the opening kickoff and Marshall recovered a fumble. Griffith, who was captain of the team, was the epitome of the Ferrum Junior College players we had been signing. He was not especially outstanding in any one area, but just a tremendous player overall. He was tough, played his heart out, and seemed to always be around the ball. Griffith's fumble recovery set up a touchdown run by Shoebridge.

During that game, we displayed our running one-two punch with halfbacks Joe Hood and Art Harris. While Joe could have played at most southern big-time programs, Harris, from New Jersey, was recruited by most major programs in the Northeast. After originally signing with Marshall, Art played his freshman year at the University of Massachusetts, sat out the 1969 season, and was back with the Thundering Herd in 1970. Both Hood and Harris did such an excellent job running the ball in the game (with each gaining over 70 yards, which was a lot for an individual back then at Marshall), Shoebridge hardly had to pass the ball. The junior quarterback added a second rushing touchdown, and our Argentinian placekicker, Marcelo

Lajterman, who was coming off of a great season on the freshman team, made a field goal.

We defeated Morehead State, 17-7, but it should have been by a wider margin. Coach Tolley and I were really proud of the defense, which gave up only 150-something total yards. From what I recall in the newspaper a few days later, it was one of the five-lowest yardage totals for an offense that particular week in all of college football. During the following week, the Marshall football program again made the news—this time, national news—but having nothing to do with our admirable on-field performance from the Saturday before.

Nearly fifty years ago when I served as a graduate assistant at Florida State, we had what were called the "Garnet and Gold Girls," females from the school helping the recruiting process as hostesses for prospects and their families. This was a relatively innovative concept for the time. I swear, the group represented one reason—although, maybe minor—why the program started to attract more highly regarded recruits by the late 1960s. Florida State still has the group, but now they are more "politically correct," and are called "Garnet and Gold *Guides*."

With the start of the 1970 season, I proposed to the university something I believed would be another way Marshall football could help its turnaround process—the "Buffalo Babes." With our cheerleaders inviting prospective girls to be part of the group, the Babes were supposed to be an organization of personable, intelligent young ladies who showed recruits and their families around campus, met visiting teams, and worked in the football office on game days. Everyone seemed to like the idea; that is, except one particular group of girls at the school. They decided to picket outside the athletic offices at Gullickson Hall the week of the Toledo game.

Protesting my idea, I recall one of the picket signs reading, "We didn't come to MU to learn to be date bait for the football team." The head of the protestors added she couldn't believe Marshall would use women to "secure" athletes, which was, and I quote, "another example of this sexist institution's systematic exploitation of . . . women." Another protestor stressed the group would be a "venture in sexism."

"Sexist," or "sexism"—it was the first time I had ever heard the words. *What the hell do these words even mean?* I thought at the time.

I was asked by a newspaper writer what I thought of the demonstrators protesting my idea. Not surprisingly, I was only partially quoted and somewhat taken out of context to say, "The ones who are out there protesting couldn't help us anyway," as if I was some kind of, well, "sexist."

I'll never forget how after the story was publicized the cheerleaders really went to bat for me, especially head cheerleader Debbie Chambers. Debbie, whose sister, Cindy, also cheered, was the daughter of a fine physician in Huntington, Dr. Joe Chambers, and his wife, Peggy. Debbie was asked by a reporter what her parents thought of the Buffalo Babes. They "like the idea" because they had heard what the group was all about directly from their daughters, Debbie said, and not from any newspaper story.

In the end, although not called the "Buffalo Babes" nor of the magnitude I originally imagined, the cheerleaders, to their credit and despite it apparently being a "venture in sexism," did start a hostess program for Marshall's athletic teams.

In our second game, we could only muster a Lajterman field goal in a 52-3 drubbing at Toledo in the rain and mud. However, we somewhat had an excuse for losing to the Rockets, who were amidst an incredible 35-game winning streak. It's been about forty-five years since, and no major college football team has won as many games in a row than that Toledo team. We won the third game of the season—an impressive 17-point victory at Xavier. Against the Musketeers, Griffith was again part of a critical fumble recovery, leading to a touchdown, and Larry Sanders clinched the game with an interception return for over 50 yards for a score. However, although our record improved to 2-1, it was becoming increasingly clear we had little depth at nearly every position, especially on both the offensive and defensive lines. And it would be only a matter of time until this lack of depth came back to haunt us.

I have always been of the opinion a team creates its own breaks, but besides having little depth, it also seemed like things often went against the 1970 team. After beating Xavier, Marshall didn't catch many breaks, and the month of October wasn't too kind to us.

A position we had considerable depth at was quarterback. Overshadowed by Shoebridge, backup signal caller

Bob Harris, who was also a junior that season, essentially came to Marshall at the wrong time. After playing for eventual Notre Dame head coach Gerry Faust at Moeller High School in Cincinnati, Bob signed with Marshall in the fall of 1968 along with two high school teammates, lineman Mark Andrews and receiver Jack Repasy. By their junior seasons, Mark was a starting offensive tackle. Jack probably had the best, surest hands on the Herd, and Bob, who would have started for most teams, backed up Shoebridge. He was considered one of the best backup quarterbacks in college football. Notably, in 1969 at Miami of Ohio and in relief, Harris set the single-game school records for both pass attempts and completions.

Shoebridge injured his shoulder in a bad loss to Western Michigan, and Bob got the starting nod at Bowling Green on Halloween. The backup was brilliant, leading us to an 11-point lead in the fourth quarter. However, the Falcons then scored a touchdown and converted a two-point play to pull within three points. Late in the game, leading 24-21, but facing fourth down inside our own 10-yard line, we decided to gamble and take an intentional safety. Marshall would still lead by a point with only the defense needing a stop for victory. However, like I said, it seemed like things often went against the 1970 team.

Leading Bowling Green 24-23 in the final minutes, we kicked off to them. In only five or six plays, the Falcons marched right down the field, and kicked about a 40-yard field goal to win the game. There may have never been anyone more pissed off than Coach Tollcy and I were after losing the game. Of course, more so than being angry simply in losing, or mad at the players, we were upset at the fact we had decided to gamble and take an intentional safety, ultimately leading to another close, frustrating defeat. During the month of October, we lost to Miami of Ohio, Louisville, and Bowling Green by just seven, two, and two points, respectively. We could have had a 4-3 record, maybe even 5-2, but were 2-5 heading into our eighth game against Kent State for our final home contest of the year.

With our NCAA probation lifted from the 1968 recruiting violations, but still serving a suspension from the MAC, we hosted a Kent State team a lot like our squad, experiencing a frustrating 2-5 campaign as well, but was much better than its overall record indicated. Shoebridge was still banged up, so Harris started at quarterback for the second consecutive game. He was going against a pretty decent Golden Flashes secondary, featuring a sophomore cornerback you've probably heard of: Nick Saban, winner of four national championships as head coach of LSU and Alabama, and probably a couple more by the time you're reading this book. Early against Kent State, Harris passed to tight end John Young for a touchdown, and Lajterman later added two field goals, but we still trailed 17-13 in the fourth quarter. Nevertheless, Joe Hood scored the game-winning touchdown on a late, two-yard run. Rushing for over 120 yards, Joe was incredible in that game with a performance that was the primary reason why we had a shot at ending the season with an even 5-5 record. Despite facing East Carolina and Ohio on the road, both were winnable games to end the season. And, a .500 record would have been a damn miracle for a football program that had struggled just to even field a team that year, at a school that was having some off-the-field troubles as well.

When I arrived at Marshall in 1968, the school had a new president, Roland Nelson, who replaced the very popular Stewart Smith. Whereas Smith was held in high regard by not only the university, but also the townspeople, Nelson appeared to make no effort to integrate himself with the students and the citizens of Huntington. At the time, this was an absolute necessity because of the turmoil in the area caused by the civil rights movement and the student unrest associated with the Vietnam War. Having never really received the level of funding from the state legislature to be a thriving university, Marshall did not even have enough money to keep the lights on—literally. During the 1970 football season, Appalachian Power had filed suit against the school, claiming it didn't pay all of its 1969–70 electric bill. However, despite the lack of funding, Marshall had strong local support while Smith was president for over twenty years, but not so much under President Nelson, who left office after only a couple of years. By the fall of 1970, thirty-eight-year-old Donald Dedmon had stepped in on an interim basis as the school searched for a new president.

With limited funding, little support from the people of Huntington (which was the biggest city in West Virginia at the time—with around 75,000 people), plus, although improving, inadequate athletic facilities, Marshall was actually lucky to have a football program at all. No wonder the Herd had experienced a 27-game non-winning streak. Considering this recipe for disaster, it was a damn miracle—and, think about this—that immediately after the long streak, we won six of the next 12 games entering our meeting with East Carolina in Greenville, with four of those losses being by a touchdown or less. Absolutely remarkable.

I guess it was because the program was moving in the right direction—revitalized, so to speak—which included the people of Huntington showing a growing interest, the football team was rewarded, in a sense. The 450-mile trip by the Thundering Herd to East Carolina was going to be traveled much differently than before.

When I coached at Marshall, every road trip was within driving distance, except to East Carolina. I'll never forget when we traveled to Greenville in 1968, and what I believe were two twin-engine DC-3s pulled up to us. I thought, holy shit, "Those planes are older than me!" And, I probably wasn't too far off. I think DC-3s were no longer being made around World War II. As far as the ride to and from East Carolina in '68, it was indeed an adventure, but no problems would arise.

For the East Carolina game two years later, athletic director Charlie Kautz was putting together a trip like none of us had experienced before. Organizing a flight itinerary that would include prominent boosters traveling with the team, Charlie was so busy the week of the game, it was almost impossible to get a hold of him. At the same time, I was in contact with Hank Norton, head football coach at Ferrum Junior College. Because of a pre-planned side trip to the Virginia school, it turns out I would not be flying with the team and its supporters.

In some ways, Ferrum football was a lifeline for us. Seven of our most prominent players were former Ferrum Panthers, including our four leading tacklers entering the East Carolina game: linebacker Art Shannon (93 tackles), defensive guard Jerry Stainback (92), defensive tackle Tom Brown (86), and linebacker Dave Griffith (73). Other Ferrum boys included starting offensive guard Pat Norrell, offensive tackle Bob Patterson, and defensive end Tom Zborill. Leading up to the East Carolina game, Coach Norton had told me about some of his second-year players—guys we would want—fitting the Ferrum mold of tough, hard hitters, who were always around the ball. In addition, he had a star linebacker who also fit the mold, plus much, much more. This particular player was *really* good, perhaps the best Norton had ever coached at the position.

Nicknamed "The Man-Eater," Billy Joe Mantooth was a six-foot-two, 215-pound monster, and still growing, junior college All-American from the small town of Clendenin, located about an hour and a half east of Huntington. Hank informed me that Mantooth was already being recruited by some big-time programs, so he suggested my recruiting trip should consist of *two* visits to Ferrum. Determined to land The Man-Eater, and after what had occurred two years before at Ferrum, I was probably willing to make 200 visits, if need be.

During my first year at Marshall, I recruited a lineman from Ferrum, who was a member of their 1968 junior college national championship team, the same season he was named the national junior college lineman of the year. I recruited him really hard, and he almost signed with Marshall. But, in the end, Rock Perdoni—the same Rock Perdoni who would be named All-American in 1969 and 1970—decided on Georgia Tech. I didn't want Mantooth to slip through our fingers and become another Rock Perdoni.

Hank suggested after I meet with the players on Thursday evening at Ferrum (which is located about halfway between Huntington and Greenville), that I return a second time, after our game at East Carolina Saturday afternoon. Evidently, the Panthers had an away game Saturday afternoon and would be arriving home that night. As their bus rolled in, I could be there waiting for my second visit in forty-eight hours.

"That would really impress the boy," Norton told me regarding a second visit with Mantooth, "and could maybe get him to go to Marshall."

So, that was that. I would not be traveling with the team either to or from East Carolina, but driving a university-issued station wagon. To show how rare it was for an assistant not to travel with the team, it was only my second, and last time I traveled separate from the players. The first time I had driven to and from somewhere in the state of Ohio. This time, Deke Brackett agreed to accompany me on the trip. Assistant coaches Mickey Jackson and Carl Kokor would miss the East Carolina game altogether, traveling to State College, Pennsylvania, to scout Ohio, who was playing at Penn State. The entire team, except a few injured players and, of course, the freshmen (who were ineligible to play) would be flying down to East Carolina. The rest of the coaching staff—Head Coach Tolley; assistants Frank Loria, Shorty Moss, and Al Carelli; and graduate assistant Gail Parker—would also be making the trip. Eleven others, who were either part of the football program, Marshall University, or media members, would be on the plane as well, including head trainer Jim Schorer, and his assistants Donald Tackett, and my "100 percenter," Roger Childers. And, finally, ten prominent, local men—a "who's who" of Huntington residents: four successful businessmen, three physicians, a dentist, a city councilman, and a member of the West Virginia legislature—made the journey. Eight of these ten men brought along their wives on the trip.

I could see why Charlie Kautz had worked so hard putting together travel plans that were nothing but first class. He was so proud, and rightfully so. Charlie had assembled a trip featuring a team that had vastly improved from one of the worst to one of the more up-and-coming programs in college football, together with some of the more respected and reputable people of Marshall and Huntington, on a chartered Southern Airways DC-9 airliner—a jet. It sure seemed a hell of a lot better way to travel than by a couple of DC-3s. The travel arrangements, as Deke would say, were 100 percent, big league.

CHAPTER 5
NO WAY THAT ANYTHING WORSE CAN HAPPEN TO US

LOOKING BACK ON IT, there were quite a number of boys originally wanting to play football at another college, but then I swooped in and talked them and their parents into choosing Marshall instead. Stuart Cottrell was one of those boys. At the time, his recruitment helped make me out to be regarded as a "good recruiter." However, in hindsight, it was one of a sequence of "sales jobs," so to speak, that I deeply regret.

Stuart was a dual-threat quarterback, an excellent defensive back, and a punter coming out of high school. He originally announced in the summer of 1969 that he would attend and play football at Kansas Wesleyan University. I visited Stuart at his home in Eustis, Florida, sat at a table with him and his family, and persuaded them to change their minds about which college Stuart would attend. I added that besides getting a good education at Marshall, he would be part of a football program that was in the process of turning things around. I also promised I would make sure to look after and take care of Stuart.

I gave the same promise to dozens of recruits and their families, many of whom were eventually members of the 1970 team.

Stuart—all 160 pounds of him soaking wet—came to Marshall and won the starting quarterback job on the '69 freshman team. As mentioned, we had plenty of depth at quarterback on the varsity the following season, so Stuart was moved to safety to back up standout Felix "Flip" Jordan. Toward the end of the season, Flip was injured and I'll admit, I wasn't too sure Stuart was first-team caliber. Boy, was I ever wrong. In his first start, at Bowling Green, he intercepted two passes. On a cool, windy afternoon at East Carolina's Ficklen Memorial Stadium, Stuart scored his first, and what would be his last, collegiate touchdown.

East Carolina, who had defeated only one team all year and was about a seven-point underdog to us, led 7-0 with about a minute and a half remaining until halftime, and were threatening to score again. The Pirates were killing our defense with a running game consisting of a one-two punch the likes I've seen few of ever since. Billy Wallace and Les Strayhorn were gashing us, each rushing for over 130 yards for the game. Surprisingly, on first down and possessing the ball just outside our 20-yard line, the Pirates elected to throw.

When Stuart intercepted the East Carolina pass, no one was between him and the end zone 80 to 85 yards away, but even if there had been, Stuart would probably still have scored. There seemed no obstacle that could ever stand in his way. Similarly to Roger Childers, Stuart always gave

100 percent on the football field, never causing any trouble and never having any issues in the classroom. He was one of my favorites, the type of all-around football player and person a coach desires. After Stuart ran back the interception more than 80 yards for a touchdown, pulling us even in a game we had no business tying, I was extremely proud of him. And, it was evident he was quite proud too. I don't think I have ever seen a bigger smile than the one Stuart displayed after reaching the sideline following his touchdown return.

Speaking of being proud, Yolanda Shoebridge is likely the most enthusiastic mother in the history of Marshall football. With her husband, Ted Sr., they sometimes traveled from Lyndhurst, New Jersey, to watch their son, Ted, play. Often ringing a cowbell, Mrs. Shoebridge let everyone know her son was quarterbacking the Thundering Herd. With Ted on the bench for the first half still nursing an injury, and backup Bob Harris struggling, the cowbell was silent. However, for the second half, Coach Tolley decided to put Ted in under center and move Bob to wide receiver. (That's how athletic Bob Harris was—he could play both quarterback and wide receiver at the college level.)

The cow bell rang loudly for the offense after halftime. Shoebridge passed for nearly 200 yards, with Harris on the receiving end of almost 100 of them in just the final two quarters of play. As always, Joe Hood was spectacular, rushing for over 100 yards and catching five passes. Still, we turned over the ball five times, were penalized a bunch, and our defense could never stop East Carolina's running attack. Marshall trailed 17-14 with less than a minute and a half to play, possessing the ball just outside its own 10-yard line.

With one last shot at victory, Shoebridge quickly moved the offense about 65 yards in five or six plays. We suddenly had the ball at East Carolina's 25-yard line with roughly 40 seconds remaining—an eternity. If worse came to worse, we were within Marcelo Lajterman's range for a tying field goal. After two incomplete passes, Shoebridge dropped back on third down and was instantly pressured. With a Pirate grabbing at his left arm, Shoebridge rolled to his right just as halfback Art Harris shredded a block. Drifting toward the sideline, a wide-open Harris raised his left arm, and Shoebridge passed to him. However, the pass fell incomplete at Harris's feet. And then, somehow, the officials dropped a penalty flag, calling intentional grounding on Shoebridge—again, for throwing the ball directly at a wide-open receiver! Our sideline was pissed beyond belief; ultimately, there went our .500 season. Facing fourth down and long from around midfield, Shoebridge couldn't connect with Hood on a long pass, and that was the ballgame.

Walking off the field, I distinctly remember thinking it was really too bad we had lost another close game, especially on a b.s. intentional grounding call, but I was proud of our team. It had some talent and a great shot at ending the season on a winning note by whipping Ohio. The following season, we'd be returning all but six or seven of our

Pictured in front of the side door of our home in Valdosta are (L to R) me, my younger brother, Rhett, and older brother, Jack, with our determined father—so determined, it was his utmost desire for his three boys to become "real" men. *(Photo courtesy of the Dawson Family)*

Here, I (right) was involved in a hard-fought game in a 48-7 win by the Valdosta Wildcats over Columbus High School at Cleveland Field during my junior year of 1958. *(Photo courtesy of the Dawson Family)*

Pictured with my father and youngest brother, Rhett, I (standing, right) am wearing my Valdosta High School letterman jacket, and proudly showing off its 1957 state championship patch. Led by first-team all-state players Bobby Hodge, Johnny Welch, and Dale Williams, Valdosta was a perfect 13-0 my sophomore year, including a 13-6 win over Rockmart High to capture the state title. *(Photo courtesy of the Dawson Family)*

nding in front of our home in Valdosta
ıy entire immediate family: (L to R) my
ther, brother Jack, me, sister Lucille,
ther Rhett, and my dad holding the
ıera (which makes me wonder who, and
ı what camera, took our picture). *(Photo*
rtesy of the Dawson Family)

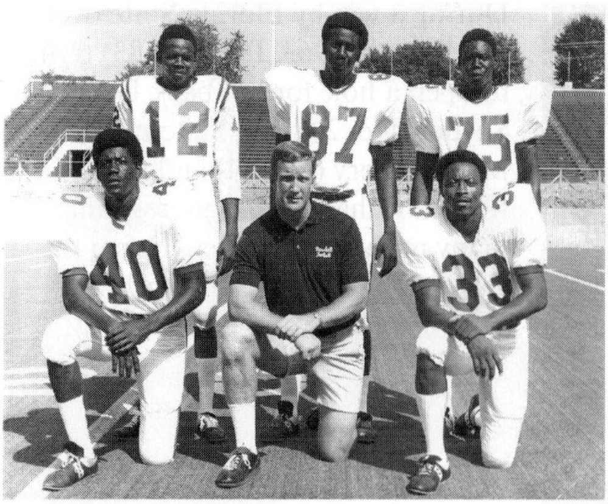

Our 1968 through 1970 signees from Druic High School in Tuscaloosa, Alabama: (Clockwise) No. 12 Reggie Oliver remains a close friend of mine today more than 45 years after his signing. No. 87 Freddy Wilson, No. 75 Robert VanHorn, No. 33 J Horn, and No. 40 Larry Sanders were all like younger brothers to me. *(Barta Studio*

Wishing everyone "Season's Greetings," the 1968 Marshall coaching staff: (standing, L to R) Pete Kondos, myself, Russ Parson, Jim "Shorty" Moss, Deke Brackett, and (sitting) head coach Perry Moss. The next season, only three of us remained; Perry Moss and Kondos were casualties of the recruiting violations, while Parson decided to sell insurance. *(Marshall University Archives)*

Marshall's 1969 coaching staff: (Standing, L R) Deke Brackett, Gene Breen, Ken O'Rourk Jim "Shorty" Moss, and Frank Loria. I'm kneeling next to head coach Rick Tolley. Afte the season, Breen, the defensive line coach, left for Virginia Tech; O'Rourke, the freshma coach, left for the Hampton (Va.) Institute. Brackett, Moss, Loria, and Tolley would perish in the plane crash. *(Marshall Universit Archives)*

I try to keep my balance during a game in 1969 on Fairfield Stadium's uneven grass field, which sloped slightly from one end zone because it was built on an old, unstable garbage dump. (Actually, I'm bending over to spit tobacco juice.) *(Dr. Joseph Chambers)*

Wearing the "100" helmet decal commemorating the 100th anniversary of the first college football game, the 1969 Marshall football team extended the program's non-winning streak to 27 games by the end of October. However, we then surprised many, including ourselves to some degree, by promptly winning three of four games in November. *(Dr. Joseph Chambers)*

)69–1970 Marshall varsity players ɔm Druid High School (Tuscaloosa, la.): From left to right, No. 87 tight ıd Freddy Wilson, No. 40 cornerback ırry Sanders, No. 33 halfback Joe orn, and No. 75 defensive lineman)bert Van Horn. As talented as they ɜre on the gridiron, these players were en better men off the field, whose lives ɜre cut way too short. *(Barta Studios)*

As senior guard Tim Bentley (No. 63) blocks, quarterback Ted Shoebridge looks to throw during the 1969 season. As only a sophomore that year playing his first season of varsity ball, Shoebridge set school single-season records for passes attempted, passes completed, touchdown passes, passing yards, and total offensive yards. *(Dr. Joseph Chambers)*

he (No. 25) demonstrates during a -7 win over East Carolina in 1969—arshall's largest margin of victory over an ponent in a 20-year period (1955–1975)—rnerback Nate Ruffin, a sophomore at the ıe, was a heavy hitter in our secondary. *r. Joseph Chambers)*

After the 1968 Druid High School (Tuscaloosa, Alabama) football team finished a perfect 10-0 coached by Lou Mims (standing left), little Marshall situated nearly 600 miles away signed likely the team's four best graduating seniors: (sitting, L to R) Flozell Horton, Robert VanHorn, Joe Hood, and Freddy Wilson. Horton, an excellent fullback, left Marshall after the '69 freshman season. The next year, VanHorn, Hood, and Wilson wouldn't get the chance to complete their first varsity year. *(Marshall University Archives)*

With head coach Rick Tolley standing in front of me during a game in 1969, I (pointing) appear rather angry at what surely must have been a bad call by the referee. Over my shoulder, defensive line coach Gene Breen looks even more upset. *(Dr. Joseph Chambers)*

As tough as Rick Tolley, or "Hard Rock," was, he was authentic, fair, and a hell of a Marshall head coach, but for not long enough—less than two seasons. More so, he was a hell of a person. *(Dr. Joseph Chambers)*

The four members of the 1970 Thundering Herd hailing from Cincinnati—all excellent players: (L to R) Juniors No. 61 offensive tackle Mark Andrews, No. 12 quarterback Bob Harris, No. 82 Jack Repasy, and sophomore No. 21 safety Felix "Flip" Jordan. *(Marshall University Archives)*

The 1970 Marshall football staff: (Back standing, L to R): Frank Loria, defensive backs; Deke Brackett, kickers and freshman coordinator; Jim "Shorty" Moss, offensive coordinator; Carl Koker, defensive line; myself, defensive coordinator; (Sitting at desk) Al Carelli, offensive line; (Front sitting on desk, L to R) Jim Schorer, head trainer; and Rick Tolley, head coach. Koker, myself, and Mickey Jackson, who joined the staff after the photo was taken, were the only ones not in the plane crash. *(Marshall University Archives)*

Joe Hood (No. 33), who I still say is the best running back I've ever seen, had quick, subtle moves which made it nearly impossible for a single defender to tackle him in the open field. Here, during our last victory before the tragedy, Hood puts a move on a Kent State defender for some of his 122 rushing yards for the afternoon. *(The Herald Dispatch)*

ching a pass at East Carolina ing what would be his final ne, Art Harris (No. 22) led rshall in both rushing yardage receptions in 1970. Tragically, ris's father, Arthur Harris Sr., nged his return-flight plans to Jersey and instead flew back his son following the game reenville, NC. *(The Herald patch)*

Whether playing on offense, in the defensive secondary, or returning kickoffs and punts, the versatile Kevin Gilmore (No. 24) seemingly could do it all. Offensively, Gilmore started at tight end, wide receiver, and halfbac during his senior season of 1970. *(The Herald Dispatch*

THE WHITE HOUSE

WASHINGTON

September 7, 1971

Dear Coach Lengyel:

There will be a deep sense of sadness as Marsha University football begins again this season, but will be mixed with warm pride that last year's freshmen have responded so positively to the gr tragedy that struck your campus.

The 1970 Varsity players could have little great tribute paid to their memory than the determina to field a team this year. Friends across the la will be rooting for you, but whatever the season brings, you have already won your greatest vict by putting the 1971 Varsity squad on the field. gratulations to you and to every member of your team.

Sincerely,

Richard Nix

Mr. Jack Lengyel
Head Football Coach
Department of Athletics
Marshall University
Post Office Box 1360
Huntington, West Virginia 25715

A week prior to the 1971 season opener, head coach Jack Lengyel received a letter from U.S. President Richard Nixon, signifying that besides Marshall enthusiasts, many more fans that year would be rooting for the Young Thundering Herd—like, an entire nation. *(Marshall University Archives)*

The 1971 Marshall coaching staff, which would supposed need a "miracle" to coach the Young Thundering Herd to just a single victory (Standing, L to R): Mickey Jackson, running backs; An Nameth, defensive line; John Riley, defensive coordinator me, quarterbacks-receivers; Carl Koker, secondary; Jim McNally, offensive coordinator; and Jack Leng head coach. (Kneeling, L to R): Graduate assistants Craig Cochran, Bill Urbani and Ron Safford. *(Marshal University Archives)*

After scoring 50 touchdowns in his junior and senior years at Portsmouth (Ohio) West High School, freshman back Terry Gardner scores his first at Marshall on "213 Bootleg Screen," defeating Xavier in 1971. The always upbeat Gardner passed away prematurely in August 2006, only a few months prior to the release of *We Are Marshall*. *(The Herald Dispatch)*

at ensued after we defeated Xavier in 1971 was a moment like I speculate few others e ever experienced in their lifetime. During the on-field chaos, I think I hugged just out everybody: offensive coordinator Jim McNally, Terry Gardner, who scored the nning touchdown, and God knows who else. *(The Herald-Dispatch)*

anity ensues on Fairfield dium's field following victory over Xavier 971. In the middle of ll, notice Rev. Robert tt, in his own words, nning like a fool," and d coach Jack Lengyel r his shoulder. *(The ald-Dispatch)*

Quarterback Reggie Oliver's (No. 12) game-winning touchdown pass to halfback Terry Gardner (No. 26) to defeat Xavier in 1971 caused nearly as much frenzy in our locker room as it did in Fairfield Stadium. *(The Herald-Dispatch)*

The miracle-working Marshall coaching staff of 1971: (Standing, L to R): Mickey Jackson, Carl Koker, me, and John Riley; (sitting, L to R) head coach Jack Lengyel, Jim McNally, and Andy Nameth. We took a group of mostly ragtag freshmen and sophomore players, who were decidedly outscored (29.9 to 5.7 points per game) and outgained (401 to 194 total yards per game), while committing an average of nearly two more turnovers per game than our opposition, and somehow won two games. *(Barta Studios)*

Accompanied by my wife at the time, Carole, while holding our three-month-old daughter, Katie, I'm one proud father at Marshall's Press Day in late summer of 1972 *(Barta Studios)*

Sitting next to me, Reggie Oliver (right), the Herd's starting quarterback the first three seasons following the tragedy (1971–1973), still attracts a crowd during autograph-photo events. After departing Marshall as the school's all-time leading passer, Reggie enjoyed a longtime coaching career on both the high school and college levels. *(Photo courtesy of the Dawson Family)*

Looking back on it, I was probably more jealous than anything else that I wasn't given the opportunity to do what I had started to do and was told I would have a chance at undertaking: rebuilding the Marshall football program as its head coach. *(Marshall University Archives)*

›ite a five-season tenure as a Marshall h (1968–1972) impaired by probation, rustration, teams losing four games for / win, and obviously the tragedy, today, I xtremely proud and grateful I was given pportunity to be a football assistant for 'hundering Herd. *(Marshall University ives)*

Even when he was the head footba
coach at Florida State, Bobby
Bowden could usually find free tim
for him and me to go golfing. In
1990, before we hit the links, we pc
for a picture. *(Photo courtesy of th
Dawson Family)*

As legendary a football coach Bobby Bowden (center) is, he has always been just as thoughtful and courteous. Only a couple of weeks after the 1993 Florida State team captured the national title, Bobby sent letters to my brother, Rhett (right), and me indicating the two of us and Fred Biletnikoff—"all of you football players"—were "as much a part of this championship as anyone." *(Photo courtesy of the Dawson Family)*

Instructed to "just look
serious," I was fortunat
be included in the *We A
Marshall* movie, playin
Morehead State head c
for Marshall's 1971 sea
opener. *(Photo courtes
Dawson Family)*

With his hair dyed red, or my *former* hair color, actor Matthew Fox (left) and I look on during filming of *We Are Marshall* in Huntington. The movie was also filmed, and completed, in Atlanta. *(Photo courtesy of the Dawson Family)*

we're "photo
ıbed" by Ned Jones
ıter), actor Matthew
and I pose just
r to the Huntington
niere of *We Are*
rshall in December
6. Actually, Ned, a
essful builder and
-time member of
West Virginia state
ıte, is a dear friend of
e. *(Photo courtesy of*
vson Family)

Pictured with me during the Hollywood premiere of *We Are Marshall* in 2006, Matthew McConaughey (right) is not only an extraordinary actor but also a really good guy. I know it's a difficult choice, but which of these two men do you think was chosen "Sexiest Man Alive" the year before by *People*? *(Photo courtesy of the Dawson Family)*

Gathering at the premier
of *We Are Marshall*
in December 2006 are
Jack Lengyel, Marshall
head coach 1971–1974,
and me flanked by the
two tad better-looking
actors who played us
in the movie, Matthew
Fox (left) and Matthew
McConaughey (right). *(*
Herald-Dispatch)

Flanked by McG (center), the director of *We Are Marshall*, and Benjamin Sandy (right), Marshall's student body president at the time, I salute the crowd at the 2006 Fountain Ceremony. For the movie, McG really immersed himself in the Huntington and Marshall community. *(Photo courtesy of the Dawson Family)*

Pictured is my lif
long friend, Rosi
(right), and me
in Hollywood in
2006. Probably, t
only reason Rosi
continues to put
with me is becau
I'm the only pers
ever to get her
into "Tinseltown
(Photo courtesy
the Dawson Fami

After years of hiding behind a sycamore tree, I finally emerged for the entirety of a Fountain Ceremony in 2006, when I was ironically asked to be the memorial's keynote speaker. *(Photo courtesy of Dawson Family)*

ginning with the duction of *We Are rshall*, I have been tinely asked to be uest speaker. I may ome emotional, or get ttle confused, like fairly ently when I called ver Luck "Oliver North" oughout a speech; ertheless, I am extremely unate and grateful I tinue to be asked back peak. *(Photo courtesy of Dawson Family)*

A few days prior to the premiere of *We Are Marshall* in Huntington, a historical marker was finally erected near the Tri-State Airport in memory of the 75 lives lost in the plane crash. *(Photo courtesy of the Dawson Family)*

For about the last decade, although there is a good chance I'll get emotional, I have found it comfortabl to be amongst and converse with the people of Marshall during the annual Fountain Ceremony. *(Marshall University Archives)*

At a recent home game, I enjoy one of my favorite Marshall football pastimes—tailgating—with two of my good friends: acclaimed Thundering Herd golf coach, Joe Feaganes, and Lucianne Kautz Call, daughter of the late Marshall athletic director Charlie Kautz. *(Photo courtesy of the Dawson Family)*

On September 9, 2011 at Spring Hill Cemete in Huntington, Mayor Kim Wolfe (right) and I (left) led a group carrying 75 American flags representing the lives lost in the 1970 Marshall plane crash be added to the more than 2,000 flags on th cemetery's "Healing Field," commemorati the lives lost on 9/11. *(The Herald-Dispatch*

24 starters; 1971 was going to be a good year. We would have a hell of a team.

I also recall spotting Coach Tolley walking off the field, and thinking, man, I bet he's *really* pissed. Rick was suddenly stopped in his tracks when a handicapped youngster approached him with a game program to sign. Rick took the program, signed it, and handed it back, with a slight smile on his face. The moment came only minutes after the discouraged, tough head coach had just suffered his fourth defeat by a touchdown or less in a little over a month. It was a moment that kind of put everything in perspective.

I remember little from the post-game experience except that a lot of people were disappointed in losing to East Carolina, and those same folks—players, coaches, administrators, and supporters—wanted to quickly get back home on the chartered DC-9 jet. As for me, as suggested by Ferrum Junior College head coach Hank Norton, I would be driving back from Greenville to Ferrum, Virginia, in an attempt to lure Billy Joe Mantooth and a few of his Panther teammates to Marshall. If Norton hadn't made the suggestion, I've wondered before if I would have driven straight back to Huntington, or left the car and flown back with the team—who knows? I'll never know.

My return trip was to be slightly different as graduate assistant Gail Parker rode with me instead of Deke Brackett. Deke wanted to get home as quickly as he could; plus, we felt the recruiting experience would be beneficial for Gail, especially since Virginia was his recruiting turf. As Gail and I started for the car, leaving the others to wait for their return trip by plane, one of my good doctor friends, Dr. Ray Hagley, called out to me, "Red, bring them home," referring to the Ferrum prospects, "We need them."

Turns out, there would be no stop in Ferrum. Past Durham and approaching Greensboro, while listening to the radio, Gail suddenly blurted, "Did you hear that?!?"

Now, I'm not sure if I heard what Gail was referring to or not; maybe I heard it, but refused to believe it. Still, I answered, "Hear what?"

Gail then explained a news bulletin interrupted what we had been listening to, saying there had been a plane crash involving the Marshall football team. We waited a couple minutes more, and the news bulletin was broadcast again: the plane had "crashed while landing" is what was said. We were staggered and terrified, but hopeful. "Crashed while landing" could mean a number of things—surely, there were some survivors; maybe everyone survived, just some injuries incurred while landing. Turns out, it was all only wishful thinking.

We stopped at the next payphone we could find to phone our wives: Gail called Jean and I called Carole. And, although neither had extensive details concerning the plane crash, both wives indicated it was more serious—*much* more serious—than what we had hoped and prayed. Carole added Dr. Dedmon, Marshall's acting president, had recently called the house, asking for me to go to the campus' main administrator building, Old Main, as soon as I got in.

Still about five hours from Huntington, Gail and I tried to get back home as quickly as we could. Both in a shock-like condition—dazed—we said very little on the drive home. We did talk some, but most of the conversation actually may have been more like conversations I was having with myself in my head—I can't remember. But, it's curious the things you do remember that occurred so long ago during such a tragic time. Sometimes, I swear, I now can barely remember the names of some good friends, but I absolutely recall—and, I have no idea why I decided to cite it—saying out loud in the car *The Funeral Lyrics* by Hank Williams, Sr. as Luke the Drifter.

I CAN'T TELL YOU where we drove, but we went out of the way somewhere. What should have taken five hours from Greensboro to Huntington took us about eight, all while driving on roads familiar to both of us. Finally, we arrived in Huntington around four o'clock in the morning. I dropped Gail off, went to my home, showered, put on a suit and tie, and rushed to Old Main.

I SOON HEARD THE tragic details of the plane crash. Occurring around 7:15 or 7:30—I honestly don't remember what time it was, nor do I really want to remember—in foggy and rainy conditions, the plane flew east across the mountains just prior to Tri-State Airport. It approached on a slope that was too low, clipped the pine trees aligning West

Virginia Route 75, and then it couldn't have taken more than two seconds before it plunged into the hillside before the runway—with absolutely no survivors.

After hearing the horrific details, I knew I would be working closely with Dr. Dedmon at Old Main for a while, getting everything organized and straightened out as best we could during the aftermath of the tragedy. I knew there would possibly be bodies to identify. So, I approached Dr. Dedmon, and told him I would do anything he wanted me to do, talk to anyone he wanted me to talk to, but I had never seen a dead person—never even been to a funeral—and I didn't think I could help with identifications. To my relief, Dedmon informed me I wouldn't have to worry about that. Three specialists in human identification—all men based at Wright-Patterson Air Force Base near Dayton, Ohio—would be identifying the bodies.

The night after the crash a community memorial mass was held at the school's Veterans Memorial Fieldhouse. About 7,000 mourners crammed into the arena to remember those who died in the plane crash. Attending the memorial was one of the toughest things I have ever had to do. Besides dealing with the obvious, it was also difficult approaching the families of the dead players who had traveled to Huntington for the service. I had to comfort them, yet a short time before, I had sat in their homes, and promised them I was going to look after and take care of their sons if they came to Marshall. I had failed on my promises.

Besides taking care of the circumstances surrounding our deceased players, we also had to take care of the forty-four players we had remaining: thirty true freshmen ineligible to play, and fourteen varsity players who were not on the plane for various reasons (eight had been held out of competition for the entire season, four were injured, and two did not make the trip because of personal reasons). This group of loyal, brave young men had approached us soon after the crash, declaring they wanted to play the final game of the season at Ohio because that's what their deceased teammates would have wanted them to do. Dedmon, along with acting athletic director Ed Starling, who was filling the role left by deceased Charlie Kautz, and myself, who had just been named acting head coach by Dedmon and Starling, deeply appreciated the boys' devotion and commitment to the program, and tribute to their fallen teammates. As we informed them, however, our football program first needed to take care of a lot of "the little things" before actually playing football again. With that being said, we also stressed the program would persevere.

On Monday morning, or it might have been that afternoon—by that time, there was no morning or afternoon in a day, just a tragic, lengthy period of time—Dr. Dedmon and I walked from Old Main to Gullickson Hall where the football offices were located. We were going to address what remained of the football team in a meeting room. I clearly remember Dr. Dedmon on the way over asking me, "What should I say? I've never spoken to a football team before."

I told Dr. Dedmon to stress that the football program would be going forward. I suspected the players were concerned Marshall football would be discontinued. It had teetered on the edge of becoming defunct fairly recently; surely, one might think, after losing nearly its entire team, it would now certainly be discontinued. I told Dedmon if he gave his guarantee the program wouldn't end, it would go a long way in encouraging the remaining players to stick around. Inside the meeting room, Dedmon indeed guaranteed the players their football program would not be shut down. I added that after what had happened two days before, there was absolutely "no way that anything worse can happen to us." After the meeting, I don't believe there was any more talk about Marshall football not moving forward.

I promptly went back to work at Old Main, trying to console families of victims over the phone and also trying to comfort families of victims who were beginning to arrive in Huntington.

We also still needed to make certain who was on the plane from Greenville to Huntington. We had an old travel roster, which listed forty-five players and nine coaches, including myself. We had a trip itinerary, but it included Gail traveling home by plane; plus, we were hearing reports that Arthur Harris Sr.—father of our standout halfback, Art Harris—had flown back with the team after flying down from Newark, New Jersey. He was to fly back to Newark following the game, but after watching his son play, altered his plans. Simply put, things had changed.

In the end, seventy-five people tragically lost their lives: thirty-five players, five coaches, eleven individuals who were either part of Marshall University, its football program, or media members, ten prominent residents of Huntington and eight of their wives, all five members of the flight crew, and Mr. Harris. Adding to the heartbreak, seventy minor children had lost a parent on that hillside; eighteen of those had lost both their mother and father.

A few days after the crash, Dr. Dedmon approached me and said there had been an issue with the identification of bodies—again, things had changed. "The police say they need someone out there helping them, Red," he said. "It's either you or me."

Dedmon explained some of the bodies had been burned or disarranged so badly that someone was needed who was familiar with the people involved with the program. He said he would go if need be, and leave me in charge of everything at Old Main, but I couldn't let that happen. Dedmon had only been active president for slightly more than four months and was unfamiliar with the football players. Assistant coaches Carl Koker and Mickey Jackson had been at Marshall about as long as Dedmon and they weren't familiar with the alumni and supporters. I didn't want to do it, but I knew then what I had to do. I told Dedmon I would help identify bodies. He said he was glad the two of us had come to an agreement because right then a state policeman was on his way to campus to pick somebody up.

For what was an absolutely awful thing to do, I was taken to the National Guard Armory at the airport, where a temporary morgue had been set up. Inside, there were tables with body bags on top, containing the remains of the dead. For the better part of a night, I identified a number of people—I still don't feel comfortable saying how many or who exactly I identified—but I identified my friends and players by their clothes, jewelry, belt buckles, etc. that remained on their bodies, plus, one or two instances by the actual appearance of a portion of their bodies.

As mentioned, it's curious the things one can remember long ago occurring during such a tragic time. . .

At some point during the identifying process, I told the forensic people I had to catch my breath—I needed a break. I walked out a side door and put in a dip of Copenhagen. From around a police car with the car tag "8154," a policeman came over and got my attention, "Hey, Red," he said just as he was pulling a bottle of beer from a sack he had. "I bet you could use this."

"I could use a few of them," I responded. The policeman then summoned a squad car to go to the store and buy some beer for anyone who could use one.

With a dip in my mouth while sipping a beer, another one of the policemen—a lieutenant—came over and asked me for some Copenhagen. I guess the lieutenant had never dipped before or, at least, not while drinking beer, because the dip, as we say, "got away" from him. The next thing you know he was puking off to the side. The lieutenant's police buddies got a kick out of that and were really laughing. I chuckled a bit for what might have been the only time I had a smile on my face during the first couple of weeks after the tragedy. However, my smile soon faded as I was summoned back into the makeshift morgue.

Worthy of mentioning, I have seen where a good number of people, mostly individuals involved in the Marshall football program at the time, have come forward over the years to claim they too identified bodies following the crash. Some have gone so far as actually *naming* the individual(s) they identified. Honestly, I find these claims difficult to believe because, for one, I don't remember seeing them there. At the National Guard Armory, I only remember observing forensic experts, people of authority including the FBI and police, doctors, and dentists. Also, I find it hard to believe the authorities would ask Marshall students/football players to help identify bodies, or the university would even allow it. Of course, as I said at the beginning, I apparently experienced some degree of repressed memory, so maybe I'm forgetting that students were involved in the identification. If not, it ticks me off that anyone would lie and say they were part of what was a difficult and horrific task, when in reality, they weren't really even there.

Back at Old Main, Dedmon and I worked day and night for about a week and a half leading up to Thanksgiving. We slept very little. I left only briefly every day to go home, take a shower, and change, and there were even a couple times I showered at Old Main. Notwithstanding, there were several others that busted their tails to help out, as well. Assistant coaches Carl Kokor, Mickey Jackson, and Gail Parker were critical in us getting through the week and a half when we had all set up shop at Old Main. There were probably others who were helpful during that tough time, but I unfortunately cannot remember who they might be.

During the day, I occasionally came outside and sat on a bench that used to be situated outside of Old Main. There, I'd sit, usually having a dip, and often crying. Around that time of year, Huntington normally has its first snowfall of the season. And, I can clearly recall sitting on that bench with the snow falling, me crying, while watching people walking around campus, most of whom were also crying. It was an eerie, surreal scene that went on for days. Marshall had cancelled classes for two days. When classes resumed on Wednesday, there were even more people walking around campus, and there I sat watching them, crying along with them. I cried so much during that time, I honestly thought at one point, I had dehydrated myself—there were no more tears left.

During the week following the crash, I remember reading in the newspaper a student quote, indicating what little good might have resulted from such a terrible situation. "Classmates were crying [together]," said the student, and then referring to the unique blending of student groups, "Long and short hair became one family."

Off campus, the scene was just as disheartening. Parents of the deceased players stayed at a motel two blocks from campus, while waiting for a phone call, indicating the FBI disaster crew had positively identified the remains of their son. This included Robert Harris, Sr. from Cincinnati, father of our starting quarterback for the three final games. Robert wrote a letter to his son on motel stationary, revealing a confidence that God would allow Bob to be with him, asking his son to never leave his side, while he waited for a phone call in quiet agony.

On Friday, November 20, almost a week after the crash, the state police announced the FBI and forensics had done all they could do. Sixty-nine of the passengers and crew had been positively identified; however, that left six unidentified. All were players: Larry Brown, Tom Zborill, Kevin Gilmore, Dave Griffith, Barry Nash, and Allen Skeens.

One of the many "little things" mentioned before that we had to do as a football program before even thinking about playing football was attend funerals. After not attending a single funeral in my first almost twenty-eight years on earth, I attended twenty-seven in a period of less than two weeks. That was a lot to attend, but for me, it was at least one funeral too few.

A joint funeral was held in Tuscaloosa, Alabama, for the four players I helped recruit while they were in high school, and we signed in 1968–1969: Larry Sanders, Joe Hood, Robert VanHorn, and Freddy Wilson. I desperately wanted to attend their funeral but was advised I was needed more at Old Main to handle arriving parents, and to attend funerals in the immediate area. Carl, Mickey, and myself planned out which funerals to attend, making sure there was at least one of us at each player's funeral. Mickey was sent to Tuscaloosa, but before he departed,

I typed a letter for him to read aloud at the memorial services. The letter in part:

> *I have heard it said that the definition of courage is "knowing the worst." I am convinced that we have "known the worst." Larry Sanders, Joe Hood, Robert VanHorn, and Fred Wilson will be forever known at Marshall University. These men, more than others, were like younger brothers to me. I know they would want us to continue our football program. We will do this with renewed enthusiasm and dedication.*

ALMOST AS DIFFICULT AS dealing with the tragedy itself and the circumstances surrounding it were the constant reminders, whether on campus or through the media, regarding the deceased, reiterating that the people we loved were gone, and were not coming back. Forty-five years later, although I've tried, the reminders have been impossible to forget.

The Ford Mustang belonging to linebacker Art Shannon, who made over 100 tackles in his only season at Marshall before he died, sat outside the university's Smith Hall. It was a tangible reminder of Art for about two weeks after the crash before his family, who lived in Greensboro, of all places, could finally come and retrieve the car. It was extremely difficult coordinating and watching the families, like Art's, coming to get the belongings of their dead sons. On television, there was a constant update as to which bodies had been identified, and which ones had yet to be identified. In the newspapers immediately after the tragedy, there was speculation of who was on board the plane. In a couple of local papers and apparently the *Miami Herald*,

I was actually listed as dying in the crash. In the papers for weeks, there were photos of the crash site, photos of the dead, speculation of who was at fault, stories of the people who perished, and stories about how their loved ones were coping with death. One story I often recall is of Pam Childers, who had been married just eight days before the crash to Marshall's "100 percenter," Roger Childers, still recovering from his brain surgery. Upon hearing Roger had been in a plane crash with the others, Pam apparently went immediately to the hospital to wait on his arrival, only to be informed no one involved in the crash would be arriving at the hospital. A couple days later, a rumor floated around Huntington that the crash had indirectly taken another life. It was reported—a rumor that was eventually dispelled—Pam had become so emotionally upset with the death of Roger, she died due to shock.

Finally, I've been routinely reminded for more than four decades, there are those individuals who weren't part of the tragedy, but if it could lead to fifteen minutes of fame, they'll claim they were. For instance—and, I don't want to come across as being too critical or negative, but I like the truth—if everyone I've heard say they "should have been on the plane" were actually supposed to be on board, but miraculously escaped death, there would have been about 400 people on the ninety-five-seat plane.

I just don't get it. There seems to be a lot of people who unjustifiably identify with being involved with the crash, wanting to be part of it, whereas I have spent a good part of my lifetime trying to forget the damn tragedy.

CHAPTER 6
A LONG, WINDING RECRUITING TRAIL

SEVERAL YEARS AGO I was traveling home to Huntington and stopped at a convenience store somewhere in the middle of West Virginia. As I was standing in line, looking through my wallet for some money, suddenly someone from behind grabbed me in a bear hug. Pinning my arms down, he then picked me up, and said softly in my ear, "When was the last time you had your ass whooped good?"

"I don't know who this is, but you feel like you're big enough to maybe whoop my ass," I replied while I was unable to see who had a hold of me. "But, I still got a little fight left in me, and if you put me down. . ."

My offender interrupted my answer by dying laughing. He put me down and gave me a big hug. With seemingly everyone in the store now looking at us, I instantly recognized the man. It was Charleston, West Virginia's Dennie Harrah, a one-time six-foot-three-and-a-half 215-pound center out of Stonewall Jackson High School, who was strong as an ox and quick as a cat. He would later be better known as the even taller, much heavier *Dennis* Harrah, who played for the Los Angeles Rams for more than a dozen years, from the mid-1970s until the late 1980s. About half of those seasons he was named to the Pro Bowl. Besides on television, I hadn't seen Dennie since I recruited him to play football at Marshall soon after the plane crash.

During Thanksgiving of 1970, immediately after the bodies were identified, the parents had been accommodated, and all the funerals were attended, with Mickey Jackson in West Virginia, Carl Koker in Ohio, Gail Parker in Virginia, and me in south Georgia and northern Florida, the Marshall coaching staff spent most of the holiday break recruiting. In fact, for the next few months, we recruited our tails off in an attempt to preserve the program while trying to keep our minds from what had tragically happened. This effort resulted in us landing some true blue chippers that winter, beginning with Dennie.

Back in Huntington after the break, it was heartwarming to experience the generous outpouring Marshall received immediately after the plane crash, and during the following weeks. Some of the tremendous support—both big and small—I can recall off the top of my head included memorial and scholarship funds set up all over the country, a sympathy letter from President Nixon, a telegram from East Carolina University desiring a "bond of friendship," a proposal from Wichita State University that the receipts it was to receive from a benefit show be shared with Marshall, a bouquet of flowers from the football team of my alma mater's hated rival—the Florida Gators, and a dollar and some-odd cents from a child who wanted to give his weekly allowance to Marshall instead of spending it on a movie.

It was the toughest of times. Although the support was deeply appreciated and certainly needed, there were additional reminders that the people I dearly cared for and loved weren't coming back. Over the years, many people have associated the crash with solely the football team when, in reality, less than half of those who died were Marshall players. I cannot begin to emphasize enough the impact that was felt by the loss of the university and community leaders in the tragedy. Besides their involvement at Marshall and with the city of Huntington, these supporters were the Thundering Herd's biggest fans, willing to travel long distances to cheer on a team who was on the losing end most of the time. Simply stated, everybody—and, I'm not exaggerating—from the Huntington area likely knew personally at least one person who died in the crash.

Carl, Mickey, Gail, another graduate assistant, Jim Gilbert, and I met after the holiday and agreed the right thing to do for Marshall was to continue to face and fight any obstacles, and with all of our might. Our primary obstacle was luring standout high school football players to Marshall after the program had gone from almost ending because of lack of interest and funding, to being on probation, to being essentially wiped out by a plane crash. It was hard enough to recruit before; now, it seemed insurmountable. But, what else were the surviving Marshall coaches supposed to do? We certainly weren't going to quit.

In January 1971, our program finally caught a break when the NCAA approved if a team was "decimated by accident or illness," as was the case with Marshall and Wichita State, freshmen were eligible to play at the varsity level (the NCAA would eventually approve freshmen eligibility for all circumstances beginning just one year later). With this new guideline, we continued to go to work, stressing to prospects not only would they likely play varsity football as just freshmen, but considering the team consisted of only several holdovers, and sophomores who had only played freshman ball, there was a possibility they could start immediately.

Over the next three months, we would sign a group of twenty-one recruits, which was not only a better recruiting class than any member of the Mid-American Conference, but a class that even rivaled some of those in the Big Ten. Besides Dennie Harrah, three other of the finest players from West Virginia committed to the squad: halfback Charles Miller, lineman Rick Sperry, and defensive tackle-fullback Jim Sanders. The notion Marshall could only sign those players West Virginia University didn't want from the state was no longer accurate in the least bit—at least not in 1971; all three of those boys were highly desired by the Mountaineers, plus, by several other major eastern programs. We also signed end Bob Witsberger from St. Clairsville, Ohio, who had turned down offers from Kentucky, Pittsburgh, Virginia Tech, and Minnesota to come to Marshall. Other out-of-state signees included four recognized on the All-American listing of *Coach & Athlete Magazine*:

halfback David Hickenbotham, lineman Tressie Dunlap, fullback Joe Wade, and offensive guard-linebacker Mike Harris.

Still, while the coaches were putting together a top-notch class, a permanent head coach had yet to be named. This was somewhat of a concern for Marshall's acting head coach of the time—yours truly.

In mid-January, my closest ally, acting President Dr. Donald Dedmon, who was in full support of me being named permanent head coach, was informed he would not continue with his role at Marshall. At the time, I was somewhat concerned a new president might not support an unfamiliar twenty-eight-year-old like myself, as Dedmon would have. Like today, a new head coach back then preferred to bring in his own assistants, so I thought there could be the possibility of me being without a job at Marshall. And, even if I was kept on as an assistant, I thought at the time, would that be fair to the new coaching regime—would it be reasonable to mix a new head coach and a few of his assistants with a few old assistants who had experienced such a tragic, life-changing event? At any rate, I continued to make a strong effort toward rebuilding Marshall, yet being open to other coaching opportunities. For example, I reached out to my old friend and coach, Perry Moss, who had become an assistant with the Chicago Bears, asking for his advice regarding my situation, and for him to keep his eyes open for any coaching opportunities. Yet, concerning Marshall's recruiting, I also checked with Perry to see if the Bears kept a list, like a lot of NFL teams did at the time, of high schools that generally produced the best football talent.

By the end of January and soon after Dr. John Barker, assistant secretary of the Southern Association of Colleges and Schools, was named president of the university, Marshall still hadn't named a head football coach. However, it was rumored Joe McMullen, a college assistant and head coach at five different schools for more than twenty years, would become Marshall's athletic director, and Sam Huff, an assistant with the Washington Redskins, the head coach. Huff, a legend in the state, had been an All-American lineman at West Virginia followed by having a Pro Football Hall of Fame career with the New York Giants and Washington. He had coached for one season with the Redskins under Vince Lombardi. As for McMullen, I knew very little about him.

Despite the rumor of Huff becoming head coach, I continued in the role of acting head coach and made plans for the upcoming 1971 season. Early on, I got in contact with my friend and teammate at Florida State, Fred Biletnikoff, who was several years into his legendary career with the Oakland Raiders, asking him to come by in the spring to work with Marshall's receivers. I was also preparing to build my staff, planning to ask my old FSU quarterback, Steve Tensi, to be an assistant if I was named head coach. Steve had just finished a six-season career in the NFL and was apparently looking to get into coaching.

In early February, McMullen was indeed named athletic director. On his first day of work, he strolled into the athletic office full of confidence and happy as could be, wearing a hat crossed between a derby and Western style, while a Sherlock Holmes–like pipe dangled from his mouth. Curiously, he passed out a pamphlet to everyone (I still have the one he gave me) titled, *"A Man with Something to Say!"—Joe H. McMullen—Vigorous! Versatile! Volatile!* It was a flier advertising McMullen as a guest speaker for church groups, schools, clubs, etc. I wondered at the time if this guy was there to be our athletic director, or to entice us to hire him as a guest speaker. McMullen kind of rubbed some people in the office the wrong way, admittedly, myself included. Here, he had made this grand, jovial entrance introducing himself to an athletic department that had recently lost nearly its entire football team. Of course, I guessed it was McMullen's way of showing that Marshall athletics needed a fresh start, and he was the man to lead the charges.

McMullen was an intriguing individual who, like me, appreciated and enjoyed poetry. He was quite the "talker," yet seemed rather approachable. During what might have been his first day on the job, McMullen likely understood how badly people wanted Marshall football to rebuild when he was approached by orphaned Debbie Chambers. Debbie, a Marshall cheerleader who, along with her sister, Cindy, had supported me during the "Buffalo Babes" ordeal, were two of the ten or so cheerleaders who had not gone on the trip to East Carolina. There simply had not been enough room on the plane for all the cheerleaders, and their protocol was if any of them could not go on a trip, none of them would go. Although Debbie and Cindy were saved from tragedy, their parents, Dr. Joe and Peggy Chambers, had been on the plane. Still, just a couple of months following the crash, representing the cheerleaders, Debbie visited McMullen, indicating she and the other girls were there in full support of the Thundering Herd, and their new athletic director.

McMullen met with the media on February 11, claiming one of the initial things he would do as Marshall's athletic director was interview me for the head coaching job. He also expected to name a new coach "within ten days."

After conducting my interview, McMullen kindly informed me of the good things I had said, while also advising me concerning things I had said that I should avoid in the follow-up interviews for the vacant job. McMullen seemed sincere and supportive, wanting to lend a helping hand to a young coach.

Soon afterward, I met with McMullen again, and he said I was one of six applicants he and the athletic committee were considering for the job. He added that of the six, I was probably the third or fourth best suited for the position. I asked if the two or three individuals in front of me didn't work out for whatever reason, would any more candidates be added to the list. He said definitely not.

A few days after McMullen met with the media, Huff announced he had withdrawn his name as a candidate for the job. Huff told the media at the time that he was "disappointed and disillusioned" with how Marshall handled his application. He said McMullen didn't like that he did not have a master's degree, and the fact he was already recruiting for Marshall before even getting the job. In the end, Huff withdrew because he felt McMullen and his relationship "would not be compatible." In the same report, McMullen indicated Huff's withdrawal left five applicants remaining.

With Huff no longer interested in the job, I started to receive support from all over to become the new head coach. I was truly honored and humbled. Letters were written to members of Marshall's athletic committee, the athletic department, and to President Barker from Marshall supporters, others in the Huntington community, and athletic staff members at other schools. A few letters I particularly recall include from Clemson athletic director Frank Howard, who had recently concluded a long, successful hall-of-fame coaching tenure with the Tigers; East Carolina athletic director Clarence Stasavich, who claimed I "would be able to give continuity to a program which Rick Tolley started"; and letters, especially appreciated and humbling, yet still heartbreaking to think about, from Frank DeBord and his wife, Marian, who each wrote one. Frank, the longtime equipment manager at Florida State and a dear friend, whose son, David, died in the crash, wrote to Marshall's chairman of the athletic committee, explaining he had recommended for his son to "go to Marshall University so he might have [the] opportunity to play [for me] and serve under [my] influence."

Near McMullen's announced 10-day hiring period, the job was offered to Penn State assistant Don Phillips. Phillips was Joe Paterno's first hire when he became head coach of the Nittany Lions in 1966. Phillips and McMullen were both assistants at Penn State together for a few seasons. After giving Phillips twenty-four hours to decide, McMullen was turned down by his one-time co-worker.

At this point, it was common knowledge around Marshall and in the media that since Phillips did not accept the job, it would be offered to Georgia Tech's Dick Bestwick, who was expected to accept the position. The forty-one-year-old Bestwick certainly had the experience, coaching three different Pennsylvania high schools to five conference championships in just eight years before becoming an assistant at the University of Pittsburgh. From there, he went to Georgia Tech, where he was a coordinator before requesting to be demoted to head freshman coach for the sole reason of wanting to manage his own program.

On Tuesday, February 23, I got a call from a writer for one of the two main Atlanta newspapers (the *Constitution* or *Journal*), asking if Bestwick had been offered the job by McMullen and/or the athletic committee. I told him I wasn't sure; I didn't know what was going on up here concerning the coaching hire. The writer then informed me that Bestwick leaving for Marshall would create an opening at Georgia Tech, and if I would be interested in that position. I told him I was always interested in bettering myself; however, I wasn't sure if I was ready to leave Huntington and Marshall. I hadn't had the time to think about it. That was it—our entire conversation.

The next day in the Atlanta newspaper, the writer quoted one of his sources from Tuesday about Bestwick and the

Marshall job: "I don't know when [Bestwick is] supposed to give [Marshall] an answer but [he] has been offered the job, Coach McMullen told me that." Obviously, if quoted accurately, the source must have been someone other than me, especially in recognizing McMullen as a "Coach."

On Thursday, I heard on the radio that the day before, Bestwick had accepted the Marshall head coaching job for several reasons, most importantly, according to him: improved facilities (the newly installed AstroTurf and remodeled Fairfield Stadium) and the athletic committee assuring Bestwick they would stand behind him. Soon after hearing the news, I was asked by a member of the athletic committee to meet with him for a "heart-to-heart," as he put it. During our meeting, the committee member gave me reasons I was actually *never* considered a viable candidate for the job: too young, lack of head-coaching experience, no master's degree, and my "harsh" on-the-field dealings with some of the players. These were the same player(s), I guessed, who felt running wind sprints was too tough.

After hearing the reasons why I wasn't a candidate, I asked the committee member why I wasn't notified of the committee's feelings back in December or January, or at least when I initially interviewed for the job. I explained how I could have had time to proactively look for a new coaching job. However, with it being as late as almost March, it was essentially impossible to find an open coaching position. It was even too late to apply for a graduate assistant position at Florida State for the 1971-72 academic year. The committee member responded by calling me a "poor loser" for wanting to leave Marshall because I didn't get the head coaching position, which was pure bullshit. Besides having poor judgement, he also didn't seem to realize I might be *forced* to leave Marshall. Perhaps, I was not in Bestwick's plans to be part of his coaching staff.

The next morning, or just a day after Bestwick agreed to be head coach, a high-ranking administrator (let's just call him) called me into his office, where I was accused of "unethically and prematurely" leaking the story of Bestwick's hiring to the Atlanta newspaper. I responded that I knew what I had told the reporter, and it wasn't what was quoted in the article. The conversation soon became heated. Apparently not listening to me, the administrator continued to call me "unethical," and "immature," and if the time came that we couldn't work together, I would be "all through." Interestingly, he ended our conversation by asking me to pick up Bestwick, and a prospective assistant of his, Dave Braine, from the Kanawha Airport in Charleston, West Virginia. He added he would do it himself, but he would be attending "rotary" (club) during that time.

Much has been said in the past about Dick Bestwick, who ultimately was the Marshall head football coach for just a few days before leaving and going back to Georgia Tech. At times, he has unfairly been associated with Marshall as the head football coach after the plane crash, who couldn't hack it, or quit, because of the tragedy, leaving for what was reported as "personal reasons" or "health issues." Nevertheless, this is what I know as the truth.

At the airport, I met Dick along with Dave, who was an assistant at the Virginia Military Institute, and was instantly impressed with both of them. On our trip to Huntington, we discussed Marshall's coaching situation and the circumstances regarding my position. I was encouraged about Dick becoming head coach, and promised him if I decided to stay at Marshall (I was still debating whether or not to try to press my luck to find another coaching job that late in the year), and if he'd have me on his staff, like I'd always done as a player or coach, I'd give him nothing less than 100 percent effort. I added that although I thought I had been unfairly treated by Marshall's athletic committee, I was absolutely not bitter about not being offered the head coaching job, especially if someone having the experience and knowledge of Dick held the position.

Regarding the athletic committee, I stressed to Dick that although I might have had a bad experience with it, he had nothing to worry about. As he had mentioned to the media when he was hired, I felt the committee indeed would support him; plus, from what I understood, none of its members would deal directly with the coaching staff anyway—that was the job of McMullen, the athletic director who, in turn, answered to President Barker.

Dick was outwardly enthused and, like any good leader, his enthusiasm soon rubbed off on others, like me. He was respectful and seemed like he would be an easy person to work under. For the first time since the tragedy, I started thinking I would be absolutely satisfied staying on at Marshall as an assistant, if it was under Dick.

That night, Dick, Dave, and I ate at a steakhouse and then watched the Thundering Herd basketball team rout Saint Francis University (PA). Throughout the evening, Dick and Dave seemed genuine, asking me to stay on with the staff. I was all on board, and then some.

The next morning, it was evident Dick had worked from his hotel room following dinner and the game, preparing for the 1971 season as Marshall University's new head football coach. He promptly called a meeting and started delegating responsibilities and thinking out loud, forming an itinerary for the next couple of months leading into spring practice. With his football playbooks spread out all across a table, Dick presented me with a new roster he had created the night before of the twenty-one players we had signed, including their height, weight, speed, etc. Just before I left to take Dave to the airport, Dick informed me that for at least the next month, besides during the day, we would need to work most nights. To me, continuing as a Marshall assistant was sounding even better and better. When I dropped Dave off at the airport, he said he'd see me in three days when he would start work that Friday.

When I returned to the athletic office, I first conducted a workout with some of the returning players, followed by watching some game film, while planning to stay as late as needed. Dick came by my desk and told me to go home; we would start working late as soon as the entire staff, including Dave and two other new assistants he had already hired, arrived on campus. Dick said he needed to make some calls, and he would see me in the morning.

On the morning of Wednesday, March 3, I got to the office by eight o'clock. An hour later, Dick had yet to arrive, but I wasn't concerned because I knew he probably had business to take care of in Huntington (he had previously informed me he had already been talking to realtors to buy a home, and was also looking to buy some local insurance). However, around eleven o'clock, the football secretary hollered for me to "come quick" because being broadcasted on the radio was a report Dick had left Marshall after just a few days on the job, and was returning to Georgia Tech.

Later the same day, a high-ranking administrator—the same one who accused me of leaking the story to the Atlanta newspaper—called a meeting. He claimed that despite him meeting with Dick for seven hours for most of the night before, trying to talk him out of leaving Marshall, he decided to return to Georgia Tech because of "family problems." He then asked me to stay afterward, and the meeting was dismissed.

For the second time in less than a week, I was accused of something I felt strongly I hadn't done. This time, I was "partially" to blame for Dick leaving Marshall. The administrator claimed Dick had said I had spoken negatively about the athletic committee. I responded by explaining what had actually been said: although I had some difficulties dealing with the committee, it would stand behind Dick, and the members said as much. Regardless, the football coaches weren't going to deal with the committee, but rather McMullen. I ended by explaining that Dick and I had agreed he and the assistant coaches could get the job done at Marshall—we could win.

"After all Dick and I talked about, how in the hell would he immediately want to leave because of an athletic committee—one he doesn't even have to answer to—that said it would stand behind him?" I asked the administrator. "Am I that persuasive?"

They were fair questions in my opinion; however, it ignited another heated exchange. Again, I was called "unethical" and "immature," and he added that it was clear I had "a lot of hang-ups." I told him it was clear he thought he knew everything, and didn't listen to the opinions of others. The administrator must not have liked my statement because he then informed me that I was "definitely" out of the running for the head coaching position. I said "I couldn't give a shit less," and even if the job was offered to me, as long as he was at Marshall, I would turn it down. He told me to be careful what I said to him. With that, I got up and said, "I won't be any trouble," and walked out of the meeting room.

Shortly after I got back to the athletic office, I found it rather ironic that broadcasted over the secretary's radio, tuned into WGNT in Huntington (now WRVC), was an "editorial comment," regarding Bestwick's departure. According to the editorial, the man who should have had the job in the first place "was already on the campus"—another humbling, appreciated show of support for me.

However, I had meant what I said to the administrator—I no longer wanted to be the head coach of Marshall and was beginning to believe I wasn't wanted by the university in any capacity.

That night, I was approached by Gail, who told me a player had informed him that some top administrators had a meeting with the players; no coaches attended. The player said the administration had decided that I had until that Friday, or less than two days, to decide whether I wanted to stay at Marshall, or leave.

The next morning, my accuser—again, the same high-ranking administrator—asked me to come to his office "for a visit." I thought he was going to simply relay to me what I had already been told—I had until Friday to decide whether to leave or stay at Marshall. Instead, I was met by a man who was all smiles who, looking back, just wanted to kick another man while he was already down—and enjoy doing it. The administrator "thought it was only fair" to inform me that in a meeting with the team, the players had asked if I would be the new head coach. When told, "no," supposedly, "all" the players stood up and began clapping. I was pretty sure this was only more bullshit being spewed. I might not have been the most popular coach, or the most well liked, but I can honestly say the players—and, probably every last one of them—respected me. As I questioned the administrator, "all the players" eventually decreased to "well, some of them." And, I still found "some" hard to believe, as well.

I asked the administrator if what I heard was true—that I had until Friday to make up my mind if I was staying or leaving. He said what I heard was true; it wasn't fair to the individuals being interviewed for the head coaching job to not know whether I wanted to be an assistant under them, or not. Keeping in mind, to everyone's knowledge only four individuals had been interviewed thus far—myself, Huff, Phillips, and Bestwick—the administrator added "a lot" of those who had interviewed said they had heard "Red Dawson was a troublemaker," and working against the program. I nearly found it humorous I was hearing such shit, but exhausted with having to deal with it.

I asked the administrator which of those interviewed had called me a "troublemaker." He would not tell me. I then asked if he only wanted to meet to tell me players had supposedly applauded when told I wasn't going to be the head coach. "I just thought you ought to know," he responded. Finally, I told him I didn't need until Friday to give him an answer. Even if I wanted to leave, where would I go? "I'm staying," I said.

More than three decades later, I spotted Dick Bestwick for the first time since he told me at Marshall University that he would see me the next morning. Having long been retired, with his last position at the University of Georgia, Dick was living in Athens, Georgia, which happens to be where Rosie lives and I visit quite often. At a Georgia basketball game, I approached him, introduced myself again, and we chatted for a while. I then asked him something I had been wondering since early March of 1971: why did he leave Marshall?

"Red, my mother always taught me that if I can't say anything nice about someone, don't say anything at all," Dick responded. Although I felt rather confident I wasn't the "someone" he spoke of, I had to ask him, "Was it me? I was blamed for running you off."

Dick paused for what was a few seconds, but it felt like an eternity, and replied, "Red, you couldn't have been nicer; it was somebody else." He then made the point that if someone accepted a job as a head coach, and that someone was really excited about the new opportunity, how would one of his own assistants run him off only after a couple of days?

Dick's perspective got me thinking. Since I had experienced over the years my fair share of people abruptly leaving better jobs than they had before, and it was never because of someone under them, but *over* them—what was promised by a boss isn't delivered, or one suddenly realizes there's probably a snowball's chance in hell that he and the boss will get along.

CHAPTER 7
THE QUITTER

I ATTRIBUTE A LOT TO how I have lived my life to my father. Before I went off to college and was living at home, my father would always want me fired up before I faced any sort of competition, whether at school, in athletics, etc. And, he could always accomplish as much by giving me a pep talk. When it was time for me to leave home after high school, realizing he wouldn't be around much to *give* me pep talks, he *left* me with one, so to speak.

Taking me to college, my daddy dropped me off in front of Florida State's Smith Hall. All I had with me was a duffel bag and a suitcase, carrying everything I owned. Right before he drove off, he handed me a sheet of paper on which the poem *The Quitter*, by Robert W. Service, was scrawled. Ever since then, I've tried to live by the so-called "code of men" and fight until the end, and never be "The Quitter."

On our drive back from Greensboro, North Carolina, when our wives informed Gail and me that the plane crash was probably worse than just "crashed while landing," the first thought to pop in my head was to run—to quit—and drive down to Valdosta instead of facing the inevitable in Huntington. What little conversation Gail and I had included discussion of the hell we would encounter once we reached home. Likewise, when accused by the high-ranking administrator of leaking the story to the newspaper, and running off Dick Bestwick, while it was clear he and members of the athletic committee didn't want me around anymore, I admittedly wanted to quit. In fact, it was hard *not* to quit, but I couldn't. Where would I go?

According to the movie *We Are Marshall*, since I was suffering with survivor's guilt from the plane crash, I temporarily left the program in 1971, and was soon asked back to be the head football coach. I turned down the job, but was eventually talked into becoming an assistant coach. In reality, although the effects of survivor's guilt had started to somewhat take its toll, the syndrome had yet to really rear its ugly head. I was mostly suffering from having to deal with the few administrators who wanted me to leave. I wanted to stay, however, and rebuild the program as either its head coach or as an assistant under Bestwick. In the end, neither job role was available, and I had no choice but to be an assistant under, at that point, who knew? It was nearing mid-March, or just one month until we were to begin spring practice, and the Thundering Herd still didn't have a head coach.

On the eleven o'clock news broadcasted Friday night, March 12, or almost exactly four months after the tragedy, I heard a head coach had finally been hired. Thirty-five year-old Jack Lengyel, who had both played and coached at Akron under Marshall's athletic director, Joe McMullen, had come from the College of Wooster—a small-college program in Ohio. At Wooster, Lengyel had taken the team from an 1-8 record his first season to a 7-2 mark in 1970 (8-1 including a forfeit) after just a handful of years. When McMullen announced the hiring, he added that although Lengyel would be bringing a few of his own assistants, the three surviving coaches—Carl Kokor, Mickey Jackson, and myself—would be retained. In addition, I was informed by the school early the next week that I would keep my coaching role as defensive coordinator.

When Jack arrived at Marshall during the middle of the following week, one thing was clear: he and his predecessor, Rick Tolley, were like night and day. Whereas Rick had been somewhat reserved and a true, tough guy, Jack was more like a college professor than a coach. He was likeable, very outgoing, and a really good speaker with an eloquent control of the English language.

I also had immediate admiration for Jack upon hearing of an ironic account of how he, in the next-to-last game of a season at Wooster, had a player, David Poetter, leave the game with a severe broken leg. After losing the game, Jack gave a brief post-game talk to his team and then immediately drove to the hospital. He stayed by the bed of the injured player the entire night. Poetter died the next morning due to complications with blood clotting. With the entire Wooster program shaken, there was some talk of the team canceling its final game of the season. Instead, Jack decided the program must press on. He dedicated the season finale to Poetter, and Wooster wound up winning. At Marshall, Jack made abundantly clear that he believed the Thundering Herd must also press on from our tragedy.

During one of my first conversations with Jack, I was told I was no longer the team's defensive coordinator. Although it hadn't been officially announced, he was bringing in his own guy, John Riley, who had been the defensive coordinator at Kent State. However, he did ask me which position I wanted to coach instead.

Granted, Jack didn't have to keep any of us—me, Carl, Mickey and, at least at that point, Gail—on staff. He could have cleaned house and brought in an entirely new staff when he was hired. However, I was a little annoyed since I was originally told I would keep the same job, but then was told otherwise by Jack only a couple days later. Although the four surviving assistants had been retained, it was evident to all of us early on that we had been somewhat pushed aside, so to speak, in favor of the new coaching regime.

Still, at that point, I decided I owed the Marshall players—the 1971 squad, and the boys who died in the plane crash—at least one season, no matter who the head coach was or the decisions he made. But, with that being said, when Jack asked me what I wanted to coach, I asked for the receivers. I felt like the receiving unit was the easiest to coach, and the easiest coaching vacancy to fill in case I ever decided to leave—like, as soon as the 1971 season is over, I thought at the time.

One week after becoming head coach, Jack officially announced his first coaching hire, Riley, and he had also decided the team's nickname would be the "*Young* Thundering Herd" for the next four seasons. Also, he concluded the Marshall football team, which would be very young and consisting primarily of players with zero varsity experience, was about to endure the "toughest rebuilding job in America." Only America? I could have added, hell, more like the *world*.

After a couple more coaching hires, Jack approached me in late March and asked if I would interview a "McNally" to possibly fill his final vacant coaching spot of offensive coordinator. McNally was even younger than I was, but an experienced coach, a great guy, and extremely enthusiastic. He had been a standout player at the University of Buffalo and then an assistant there for several years before the program was discontinued. Jack and I both agreed McNally would be a great hire, and a hell of a coach, and likely for many years to come. I must say we were correct in our assessment: Jim McNally coached for more than 40 consecutive seasons, during which time he made eight different stops, before his retirement in 2007. This included 28 seasons in the NFL as the offensive line coach for four different teams.

In early April only about a week before the beginning of spring practice, Jack decided we needed to scrap the pro-style offense Marshall had been running, and implement the Veer. The Houston Veer, or Wishbone-T, was similar to today's triple-option offensive attack. Back then, the notion was if your offensive players, on the whole, were rather quick, but smaller and not as athletic as the opposing defensive players—if the opposing defense "out-personneled" your offense—the Veer was probably a good option. The Veer spreads out a defense, allowing a team, instead of running through defenders, to run around or between them. As Jack said, Marshall could "do the most-est with the least-est" by implementing the Veer.

We soon reached out to my ole Florida State buddy and coach, Bobby Bowden, who had just completed his first season as West Virginia's head coach after serving as its offensive coordinator. We asked him to help us get back on our feet by teaching us the Veer. In both 1969 and 1970, Bobby's Veer had been one of the top offenses in major college football. We were desperate, followed by being extremely grateful, because we knew we weren't going to out-personnel anybody on our schedule that season. So, Jack, myself, and the two other offensive assistants headed to Morgantown to pore over playbooks and game film for three days, learning our new offense. Notably, also while at West Virginia, which had started its spring practice in late March, we noticed the Mountaineers had placed a green cross on the backside of their helmets, wearing them the rest of spring to honor the victims of the crash.

At Marshall, there once had been a joke that the only thing worth publicizing about the university was that famous comedian Soupy Sales, and Hal Greer, who was beginning to wind down a hall-of-fame basketball career, were alumni. That certainly wasn't the case anymore by mid-April of 1971, when media members nationwide traveled to Huntington to witness the Young Thundering Herd take the field on a Tuesday for the first spring practice.

Although, in some way, the rebirth of Marshall football had actually begun transpiring the day before when a single family traveled to Huntington from New Jersey.

Having not been at Fairfield Stadium since they witnessed their "Teddy" quarterback Marshall to a season-opening win over Morehead State seven months before, father, Ted Sr., mother, Yolanda, and youngest brother, Terry, returned to the place where Ted Shoebridge had starred for the Thundering Herd. Except this time, Yolanda wasn't carrying the cowbell like before to "ring on" the team, but a floral memorial to place at the stadium to pay respects to those who died on the team. Stalling for just one more day until practice officially started, I still couldn't bring myself to enter the stadium. However, I was told Yolanda wanted me to take her to the crash site. Although reluctant, and not knowing how on earth I would make it through viewing the hillside where many of my friends' lives had ended, I couldn't say "no" to a mother's desire to see where her son had been prematurely taken by the Old Master. Afterward, the Shoebridges made their way to Huntington's Spring Hill Cemetery where the six boys in the crash who could not be positively identified were jointly buried, including Ted's roommate, Kevin Gilmore.

The next afternoon, I walked into Fairfield Stadium for the first time since November 11—the Wednesday practice before the team had departed for East Carolina. This group of seven coaches, three graduate assistants, and about forty-five players, nearly all of whom were freshmen-turning-sophomores, or walk-ons, manifested a series of mixed emotions. There were the upbeat, like Jack, who kept saying things like the job was a "once-in-a-lifetime opportunity," "the Young Thundering Herd is on the way back," and his goal was to go 10 and 0; the wide-eyed, like most of the players on that field, who really didn't know what the hell to think or expect; the disheartened, like myself, who couldn't keep focused on the new team, but kept being reminded of the squad from the previous season; and finally there was the damn media, who were looking for some sort of story. A particular member of the media overheard a quote for his story—something I now wish I had never said—when I confessed to another coach, "There's a million places I'd rather be than here today. You name the place and I'd rather be there."

To open spring ball, the team was led onto the field by the three surviving letterwinners from the 1970 team—Felix Jordan, Ed Carter, and Nate Ruffin—and end Pete Naputano, a junior-college transfer the season before who had been injured and didn't make the trip to East Carolina. Joining them were several guys who had quit the program prior to the tragedy, but had returned primarily because they believed they owed their deceased teammates a second try. Others included linebacker Dave Smith, who had been a standout on the Marshall *basketball* team, averaging more than 10 rebounds per game for each of his three seasons on varsity. Freshman Sidney Bell, who arrived on campus the previous winter from the Virgin Islands wearing beads, baubles, and a free-flowing Caribbean shirt, was such a good basketball player, he had played for his country's national team in the Pan American Games. Lining up at receiver that spring, Sidney became the first-ever college football player hailing from St. Thomas. Offensive tackle Jack Crabtree, whose life was essentially spared from the crash because of poor grades, was also returning. Before the start of the 1970 season, Crabtree became academically ineligible. The sophomore, who was married with two small children, was back to get an education while making a second attempt at college football.

Absent on the opening day of spring practice was a sports information director, a team physician, head of the Big Green Club, and managers/trainers familiar with the program—positions that had previously been held by those who died in the crash, and had yet to be filled. We had a team manager, but he was new and had no idea how to distribute the uniforms and equipment. He asked Jack, who said to start by giving it out to the seniors, then the juniors, and so forth. To which, the manager replied, "But, everyone's a freshman!"

For twenty spring practices over the course of thirty-five days, overtly, there could be some strong friction among the few of us who couldn't keep the tragedy out of our minds. One of the things *We Are Marshall* was spot-on as far as the reality of the movie was its portrayal of the conflict that persisted between Nate Ruffin and me. Nate, a senior defensive back in 1971, was one of the biggest hitters on the team, and could have possibly played professionally on some level. In the spring, evidently overwhelmed with the sadness and anger of losing many of his friends, Nate took his aggression out on his own teammates, most of whom he hadn't played with before, with blind-siding, late, and unnecessary hits. In one scene, after an unnecessary hit by Nate, the movie shows actor Matthew Fox hollering at Anthony Mackie, who played Nate, asking if because of the tragedy, Nate was the only one who had a right to be pissed off—the only one who had it rough. A similar scene actually occurred that spring between Nate and me at least a half-dozen times. Because of the tragedy, yes, he did have it rough, but so did everyone else who knew the people on the plane. Although I might not have handled Nate's outbursts in the best way, I was not about to allow him to injure his own teammates, especially since we hardly had any players as it was.

Even though we were allowing just about anyone to join the team (if you were a Marshall student and wanted to play football for the Young Thundering Herd, you could), we still had so few kids toward the end of spring practice. We often had to scrimmage the first-team offense against the first-team defense. Because of the possibility of having more injuries occur, this is something a team rarely, if ever, wants to do.

Although a very spirited bunch, our ragtag group of players at the end of spring consisted of probably only about a dozen who could have been considered legitimate college football players. We were so undermanned that we actually had fewer players than our opponent for the sixth annual Green and White game in mid-March matching the Varsity against an alumni squad. In fact, the Varsity was so much lacking in skill, a lot of us thought we'd actually get beaten by the Alumni team, coached by McMullen, which had never won the spring game in five tries.

The Varsity squad, coached by Lengyel and consisting almost entirely of players who had never played a single down of Varsity ball at Marshall, capped spring practice by playing its first game in more than six months in front of 4,500 spectators at Fairfield Stadium. Taking a critical step in the right direction, and what could still be the most important spring game for a program in the history of college football, the Varsity routed the Alumni, 26-0. Standouts for the Varsity were all members of the freshman team the year before: sophomores David Walsh, Steve Johnson, and John Johnstonbaugh, who originally wasn't a scholarship player. Johnstonbaugh rushed for over 100 yards, Johnson intercepted three passes, and Walsh was brilliant engineering the Veer offense, which picked up nearly 450 yards compared to the Alumni's roughly 150.

Coaching the quarterbacks at this time, along with the receivers, and calling most of the plays, I was really proud of David. He passed for more than 150 yards and three touchdowns, while picking up about another 40 yards rushing. The only real downside to our performance was our placekicking. Going for two points following each of our four touchdowns, we didn't even attempt a point-after kick simply because we didn't have a legitimate placekicker to do so.

The days following the spring game and leading up to the regular season was a really difficult period for me. I couldn't keep the tragedy off my mind and evidently it showed. In one case, an administrator stopped me during the summer and told me I needed to "forget" the tragedy. Soon afterward, *another* administrator told me, "You got to forget it, Red, and move on." I didn't really respond in either case. Finally, after hearing as much for about the fourth time that summer—a couple times from each administrator—I became fed up with hearing how I needed to forget the tragedy. And I blew up.

"That's the second time you've said that!" I shouted at the administrator. "I knew seventy of the seventy-five people on that plane! Tell me how am I going to forget that! Please, teach me!" I added sarcastically.

I eventually went on a much-needed, week-long vacation that summer. When I returned, there was a contract on my desk for the 1971-72 academic year. When I looked to sign the contract, I noticed its deadline date was *during* my vacation. In other words, a contract was left on my desk while I was on vacation with a deadline date ending just a couple of days later while I was still on vacation. When I approached the high-ranking administrator about my circumstances, he said there was nothing that could be done and, without a contract I was not legally employed by the state. Well, I knew some other higher-ups at Marshall who actually supported me. I immediately called one of them, received a contract the next day with an extended deadline, and thus rightfully became legally employed by the state.

If it wasn't abundantly clear before, it should have been then that there were certain higher-ups at Marshall who wanted me gone, but didn't have the grounds to stand on to get rid of me. So, they were going to try to force me out. Why did I stay? At that point, it was really no longer about not being able to find a job. I could have found *some* job during the summer of 1971. It probably would not have been in coaching, but I was actually beginning to question if I still enjoyed coaching, especially after all I had been through. I put up with the harassment because I had promised many families, from those of newly signed recruits to those whose sons had died in the crash, like the Shoebridges, that I would stay at Marshall and help build the football program in memory of the perished team. Although disgruntled with some of its administration, I certainly loved Marshall, and wanted to help lay the foundation to what we had started to build prior to the crash.

Gail, one of the few of us remaining, who had helped build the program prior to the crash, and then was laying its foundation again in 1971, was suddenly and unfortunately dismissed that summer. He had gone through spring practice and into the summer, and wanted to remain at Marshall, but wasn't retained as a graduate assistant. Jack decided to bring in his own guys, and that left Gail without a position at Marshall. Because of all Gail and I had been through—together—I was upset. He was a hell of a coach, and an even better person. However, as is sometimes the case, the graduate assistants are the first to go when a new coaching staff comes in although, might I add, not normally *months* after the new head coach has arrived. The most difficult part of Gail's departure was we agreed just before he left that we should probably not see one another in person in the immediate future, and maybe forever. Although difficult to fully explain, we agreed seeing one another would invoke many bad memories and be too damn painful for the both of us.

During the summer and leading up to fall camp, Gail wasn't the only one to leave the program. When our new signees were finalized in late June, we had lost nine of the twenty-one newcomers Carl, Mickey, Gail, and I had initially signed by mid-February. Similarly to graduate assistants often not being retained by a new head coach, it was a negative side of college football. Prospects often sign with a particular school based on the head coach and his assistants. And when there is suddenly a new head coach, bringing in new and unfamiliar assistants, those same prospects will often change their minds and sign with the programs that had originally been their second-best choice. Unfortunately for Marshall that summer, the nine prospects we lost may have been the nine best of the original twenty-one signees. Departures included highly recruited out-of-state players such as end Bob Witsberger, halfback David Hickenbotham, lineman Tressie Dunlap, fullback Joe Wade, and offensive guard-linebacker Mike Harris. In-state signees halfback Charles Miller and defensive tackle-fullback Jim Sanders left for West Virginia University, while lineman Rick Sperry flipped to rival and season-opening foe Morehead State. And, perhaps the worst loss of all was first-team All-State center Dennie Harrah, who decided instead to attend the University of Miami in Florida.

The Marshall coaching staff would do an excellent job of recovering from what we lost in quality, gaining in quantity—which is what we really needed. In the end, we signed thirty-six recruits, including twelve of the original signees. And, although all the blue chippers had left, some young talent still remained, like Charles Henry. Charles was a five-foot-eleven, 180-pound linebacker from Conway, South Carolina. He and *Coach & Athlete* All-American Tressie Dunlap originally signed with Marshall from the same high school. By the summer, Dunlap had left, Charles remained. Although small, Charles was a good hustler, always around the ball, and maybe the quickest linebacker I had seen on film all year. We weren't the only school that wanted him—so did some big programs, like the University of Maryland, who wanted Charles to first attend a junior college, but he could play immediately at Marshall, and likely start at the mere age of seventeen.

I don't want to take anything away from the two dozen recruits we signed after nearly half of the original signees opted to attend other schools. There's an excellent chance we would have pursued them regardless, like halfback Terry Gardner. Terry, a speedster from Portsmouth, Ohio, scored 60 touchdowns in high school, was selected to play in the state's esteemed North-South all-star game, and got a scholarship offer from Ohio State. He reminded me of some of the upbeat, really athletic players involved in the tragedy—always a smile on his face, tremendous attitude, and having a "motor" that ran as fast as his legs carried him.

In addition, a number of walk-ons appeared like they would compete for playing time, like freshman defensive lineman Dan Norrell. Dan was the younger brother by several years of Pat "Nutsy" Norrell, an outstanding offensive guard who died in the crash. Dan, who attended high school in New York, had said he knew he wanted to walk on at Marshall two weeks prior to the crash when, visiting Pat on campus, he was told by his brother he'd love it there; the people at Marshall were his "kind of people." Finally, we were provided with even more support when four or five players followed assistant coach McNally from Buffalo's dormant program, and a few of them appeared like they'd start immediately on defense: linebacker Dave Homa, end Pete Diabo, and cornerback Gene Nance—the younger brother of the great fullback Jim Nance, who was a teammate of mine with the Boston Patriots.

As Marshall opened fall camp in mid-August, we were regarded in the media as a "collection of players without stars." Despite having few standouts, we certainly had quite the "collection"—nearly 100 players altogether. However, as camp began to unfold, we ran into the same problem the coaching staff encountered when I had first arrived at Marshall three years before.

Whereas some newcomers thought fall camp was too tough, as before, others were suffering from homesickness. Altogether, we lost seven signees before the season had even kicked off. Of the remaining signees, only a couple were from Ferrum Junior College—a one-time pipeline to Marshall. Needless to say, this did not include the prospect

Gail and I had originally planned to visit a second time on our way back from East Carolina—linebacker Billy Joe Mantooth, who had decided to attend West Virginia. We would have had even more guys leave, but we'd occasionally get a call during camp from a player at the dorm, indicating a newcomer was packing his bags and planning to leave. One of us coaches would then run to the dormitory, and help the youngster unpack his bags; we couldn't afford for another one to leave.

In addition to the handful of signees leaving the program, we had some veterans unfortunately do the same. From mid-May's spring game, five Varsity starters—not players, *starters*—left Marshall for various reasons leading up to the season opener. The departure of key veterans was among the reasons why it seemed we spent a great deal of summer practice moving guys around and trying them out at different positions, mainly switching incoming freshmen from the offensive side of the ball to defense. More than one-third of our twenty-nine remaining signees wound up moving to a new position from where they were originally slotted when they arrived on campus. And, I'm not talking "moving positions" like a fullback to tailback but, more like, tight end to defensive guard, halfback to defensive back, center to defensive end, and so forth.

One of those incoming players, who was forced to switch positions, remains a great friend of mine today (but, probably only because I named a drill after him, and I sometimes mention it whenever I give a speech). At six-foot-three and running a 40-yard dash time at under

4.6, Roy Tabb came to us from Hayes, Virginia, as an all-district halfback and defensive back; however, since he had the perfect lanky body and athleticism to be a wide-out, he was moved to my receiving unit during the summer. Despite all of his talent, Roy often "heard footsteps" when a pass was thrown to him. As the ball approached, he flinched, thinking more about the oncoming defensive back(s) rather than the thrown pass, and usually dropped the ball. So, I created the "Roy Tabb Drill" during fall camp of 1971.

The drill began with Roy facing me, standing still. I'd send another player to run directly at him from the side. I'd then fire a pass directly at Roy and, just before the player squared up to make a hit, the ball would hit Roy right in the hands—and would be routinely dropped. No telling how many times we ran the drill over and over, resulting mostly in dropped balls, until I decided to add a twist to the drill—encouragement.

"Roy!" I hollered one practice. "You want me to make you a better pass receiver, right?"

"Yes, sir," he said.

"Okay, so what's going to happen if you keep flinching and dropping the football?" I asked.

"I'm probably not going to play," he replied.

"That's it! And, what's going to happen regardless whether you flinch and drop the ball, or not flinch and catch the ball?" I asked.

"I'm probably still going to get hit," he answered.

"Exactly, you got it! Now, let's run it again."

From then on during fall camp, when we ran the Roy Tabb Drill, Roy and I would have a similar exchange. Wouldn't you know, by the end of camp, he could catch the damn ball in a crowd with the best of them because, as Roy himself discovered on his own, he was going to get hit whether he caught the ball or dropped it. And, if he continued to drop it, he wouldn't play, but Roy wanted to play very badly. He entered his true freshman year as likely Marshall's second-best receiver, only behind all-everything Lanny Steed, one of our original twenty-one signees. Steed was so talented in high school, he was named to the All-Kanawha Valley team—the same recognition earned by Dennie Harrah—except, Lanny was honored at *two* positions, halfback *and* defensive back.

More than thirty years later, when I would speak to groups on "leadership," I would stress that a good leader can find productivity—in something—in anybody they are guiding, teaching, coaching, etc. Sometimes repeatedly running them through "the drill" doesn't work; they need encouragement as well. And here's the key, a leader gets into the mind of the learner making them think what the leader wants them to think, and often allowing them to believe they came up with the notion on their own.

By the time we were preparing for Morehead State in mid-September, with some encouragement, Roy Tabb believed he had discovered how to catch a football in traffic, and the consequences if he dropped it. Concerning all of the Marshall players, who in all honesty, would have probably struggled to defeat some top-notch high school teams, there was plenty of encouragement, and Jack had them believing it would win—not "10 and 0" like he forecasted very optimistically, but we sure in hell weren't going 0 and 10. As far as any consequences, there was severe disappointment if, by chance, we did not succeed in front of a growing fan base and as the nation's eyes watched closely to see if the team that practically lost all of its players and coaches could rebound from tragedy.

CHAPTER 8
THE BEGINNING

LONG BEFORE HE BECAME a record-breaking wide receiver, Super Bowl MVP and hall of famer Fred Biletnikoff impressed me. The son of Russian immigrants, Fred grew up in Pennsylvania, and still carries a distinctive, articulate accent, much different than my southern drawl. While at Florida State, although we were rather opposite to one another, we were close friends and still keep in touch. Maybe opposites *do* attract, as they say, or maybe we became close because neither of us ever had any money at the time.

Don Fauls, the well-respected trainer for the Seminoles, and his wife, Marg, were like parents to Fred and me. They looked after us and even allowed us to bring our dates over to their house. Don and Marg knew Fred and I had little money to take our dates anywhere else, so they would give us ice cream, soft drinks, and the like, and talk with us. Fred and I had a saying for what we called "Fauls' Drive-In," where it's "a little out of the way, but a lot less to pay."

On the practice field, I believed early on in our FSU careers that if I worked hard enough, I could actually be a better player than Fred. This was based on the belief I had developed early in life: if you work harder than the other guy, you'll be better than him. What made Fred Biletnikoff different than the "other guy"? Well, here's just one simple example:

In 1964 Florida State lost only one game the entire season: a 20-11 setback to a very average Virginia Tech team. It was a bad loss where pretty much everybody for the Seminoles played like crap, except Fred, who was spectacular even in defeat. We gained more than twice the number of total yards than the Hokies had: 420-something to around 190 but, as far as those all-important turnovers, we committed three while forcing none. Fred, by himself, having just 12 touches (receptions + rushes) gained 188 yards, or nearly as many as the *entire* Virginia Tech offense.

Because of Fred, I learned that in life, there are times the gifted will always be better than the "other guy" no matter how hard the latter works. Accordingly, I also learned that I better start getting used to being regarded as Florida State's "other end."

As mentioned earlier, during the winter of 1970-71, when I was supposedly Marshall's acting head coach, I asked Fred to visit us that spring to work with our receivers. Besides planning to approach Steve Tensi, I had also already received a coaching commitment from Frank Vincent, who had just won three West Virginia state championships in a row at Charleston High School (1968-1970).

In this case, besides learning from my fellow FSU end that very hard work doesn't always triumph over talent, Fred was also part of another valuable lesson: one should never plan *too* far in advance. Situated in the foothills of the Appalachian Mountains in northeast Kentucky, I couldn't help but think how I had worked so hard, and persistently planned as Marshall's acting head coach, hopeful of becoming the permanent head coach, but there I sat in the press box at Morehead State's Jayne Stadium calling plays, having been informed I had never actually been the head coach of any type. Although the acting president and athletic director at the time had told me otherwise, maybe there was something to it. Leading up to our season opener, along with reading it would be a "miracle" for us to win a single game in 1971, it was said our final signing class wasn't "particularly good" partly because Marshall had been "without a head coach for nearly five months." Nevertheless, I had promised mommas, daddies, and their sons, I would help build—for a second time—the Marshall football program; therefore, I was going to give 100 percent effort in doing so, regarless of my exact role with the team. To win a game that season—to pull off a "miracle"—we were going to need 100 percent effort from a good many folks.

Our fan base gave 110 percent leading up to the opener. For the 1971 season, Marshall's season ticket sales were at an all-time high. In addition, roughly 4,000 Young Thundering Herd fans drove more than an hour to Morehead, actually increasing Jayne Stadium's capacity attendance from 10,000 to about a thousand more. And, of the Eagles fans there, I honestly think a portion of them were rooting for us. Hell, the entire country was rooting for us—the destitute football program, featuring more than seventy freshmen and sophomores of its eighty-something players, given little chance to succeed—even for one time, just a single victory.

I'll never forget what a Marshall fan said following the 29-6 loss that night to Morehead State: "I just wanted to see them trot out onto the field and play." Personally, although I had mixed feelings at the time, I will forever be proud I was part of "them"—*that* team.

Although Morehead State beat us badly, and it actually could have been worse, our ragtag bunch of newcomers did okay that night. We were outgained in total yardage something like 450 to 140. But Morehead State lost four fumbles and had two touchdowns called back, and Marshall trailed only 16-6 entering the final quarter. The Eagles' quarterback, Dave Schaetzke, was a dual threat who was difficult to stop. He completed more than half of his 20 passes or so, rushed for nearly 100 yards, and was responsible for two touchdowns. Schartzke said following the game it felt like the entire crowd was rooting for Marshall, and he was right. Beginning when we walked out onto the field when the crowd rose to their feet, to what seemed like after every play when they applauded, it remains the only football game I've ever experienced where the away team seemed like the home team.

One of the few on-field bright spots for Marshall against Morehead State was the play of Reggie Oliver. Reggie, a sophomore who was the only surviving player of the five boys we signed from Druid High School in Tuscaloosa,

Alabama, had been a two-time all-county quarterback but was switched to wide receiver soon after he got to college because of our depth at the positions and his athleticism. He had started at split end in the spring game; however, as fall camp started, it became evident none of the few quarterbacks we had were a perfect fit to run the Veer offense. Reggie gave it a shot and really excelled, eventually surpassing Dave Walsh as the number-one quarterback less than a week before the opener. Against Morehead State, Reggie completed half of his dozen or so passes without an interception, including throwing for our lone points—a touchdown pass to sophomore tight end Tom Smyth about midway through the third quarter. For Smyth, it was the first time he had ever scored a touchdown. For Marshall, the seemingly insignificant touchdown showed everyone—players, coaches, fans, and any doubters—at least we could score points.

Placekicking, however, continued to be an issue. In the first half, our offense had driven inside the opponent's 10-yard line before stalling. We called on our primary, and Marshall's only placekicker—a guy I recall who kicked barefooted. He missed a field goal wide from 20-something-yards out. Later, after the Reggie-to-Tom scoring pass, I cannot recall if we went for two points to cut the Musketeers' lead to a touchdown and a two-point conversion, or if we did so because it was assumed our kicker would probably miss a point-after kick. Regardless, our try for two points was unsuccessful.

After the Morehead State game, the barefooted placekicker quit. I'm guessing he did so because he couldn't make a short field goal, and the lack of confidence we had in him even making extra-point attempts. So, Jack put a story in the school newspaper advertising an open tryout for our placekicking position. A scruffy-looking former soccer player from New York State, Blake Smith, tried out, having never played football, never put on a football uniform, and never even seen a football game in person. Because of his extreme unfamiliarity with the sport of football, it was rather fitting Blake won a tryout for the most inexperienced team in all of college football. Jack told him he could be the Young Thundering Herd's placekicker under one condition: if he cut his damn scruffy hair and shaved. Blake did so, and we had ourselves a kicker again.

The week of the Xavier game, we were so beat up and lacking adequate depth that at one particular practice, the only players who scrimmaged were the ones who saw little to no playing time at Morehead, while everyone else went through light drills. Since we were facing a school located in Cincinnati, it was decided the game captains would be our two players hailing from The Queen City—Tom, the tight end, and standout defensive back Felix "Flip" Jordan. As far as who was going to start at quarterback, that wasn't as easy of a decision.

Staying true to the run-oriented Veer offense, we attempted less than 20 passes against Morehead. However, if our offense had any chance to move the football against Xavier, we were going to have to pass more—at least twice as much as the week before. Between our top two quarterbacks, Reggie directed our offense better and was a little bit better of a runner, but Dave was more of a drop-back passer. In the end—like, only ten minutes prior to kick-off—Jack decided to go with Reggie.

Without getting emotional myself, it's difficult for me to describe the emotion I felt while running out onto Fairfield Stadium for our first home game since the tragedy. The stands were packed with more than 13,000 spectators, including the state governor, Arch A. Moore, and the parents of the late Rick Tolley. Reggie later claimed the crowd sounded like a sudden burst of thunder when we emerged from the dressing room, and there's no better way to describe it—an instant *boom*! What makes the roaring even more remarkable is that a good portion of the crowd couldn't cheer, but could only cry—some literally sobbing—at the mere sight of Marshall football's return home.

After the American flag was raised at Fairfield—the same one that flew over the State Capitol the day after the plane crash—the game kicked off just before two o'clock in the afternoon. The entire first half was a defensive battle with the lone score coming as the first quarter ended when Blake made a 31-yard field goal. To illustrate how noteworthy his field goal was, not only had Blake, who wasn't even wearing shoulder pads, kicked a football for the first time in his life only four days before, but whether attempted by Blake or two other kickers we used in 1971, Marshall attempted six other combined point-after kicks and field goals that season, and did not make a single one.

The turbulent crowd was treated to quite the halftime show. We still had that live buffalo as a mascot, Marco, who still wasn't trained to act appropriately on the field. He got loose during halftime and Jack, who I'm guessing felt especially upbeat since we had a shocking 3-0 lead at the time, tried to contain him. Needless to say, Jack did about as good a job of grabbing Marco as I had a little over a year before with Dr. Pete Proctor at the fairgrounds.

Both teams moved the ball well in the second half. In the third quarter, Xavier scored on a short rushing touchdown to cap a long drive. The Musketeers missed the PAT. We eventually answered early in the final quarter, when Reggie drove Marshall more than 70 yards, ending on a short touchdown run by the quarterback. Reggie was unbelievable that game, completing 20 of 43 passes for 240 yards, and at least 10 of his incompletions were dropped balls. Ironically, his completions and pass attempts both tied single-game school records at the time held by his deceased teammates, Bob Harris and Ted Shoebridge, respectively.

Leading 9-6, Reggie bruised his elbow on our next possession and had to leave the game. In relief, Dave couldn't move the offense for the next two or three drives, but Xavier couldn't move the ball either. Only four minutes away from an improbable victory, we were forced to punt from deep in our own territory. And then, it happened, and by an opposing player whose name I'll never forget—John Gompers. Xavier's Gompers appeared to have ruined our "football fairy tale," when he grabbed a Bob Ensbaugh punt around midfield and raced for a touchdown, giving the Musketeers a 13-9 lead and what looked like the ballgame. Our roaring crowd instantly turned silent.

A win really seemed unlikely when Dave couldn't move us on the ensuing possession, and we were forced to punt again; however, the Herd defense, which really played lights-out that afternoon, then stood its ground and forced the tenth Xavier punt of the game.

Down by four points, possessing the ball on Xavier's 48-yard line with only 1:18 remaining, I called down to offensive coordinator Jim McNally and we agreed: regardless of his injury, Reggie Oliver needed to take the ice off his elbow and get his butt back in the game. No offense to Dave; he was to Reggie what Harris had been to Shoebridge, a more than capable backup, but he wasn't going to lead the team—not then—about 50 yards downfield in only 78 seconds. Jack conceded and Reggie went back in for the first time since early in the quarter.

I was more than second-guessing myself after Reggie threw incomplete on our first three plays. However, on fourth and 10, he passed for 11 yards to receiver Jerry Arrasmith, a sophomore from Kentucky. On the next play, Reggie threw for another 11 yards to receiver Kelly Sherwood, the younger brother of West Virginia quarterback great, Mike Sherwood. From Xavier's 26-yard line, Reggie threw incomplete twice before hooking up with Arrasmith again for 13 yards and a first down to the 13-yard line. Just a few years before, college football had adopted the rule that the clock stopped after gaining a first down, and thank goodness for that right then. However, Jerry wasn't able to get out of bounds to completely stop the clock until we snapped the ball the next play. Instead, the clock would only be stopped long enough to move the chains, then restarted again, and there was only a handful of seconds remaining. However, it would be stopped just long enough for me to think the situation through.

As Reggie and the rest of the offense raced to the line of scrimmage with no timeouts remaining, I knew we had enough time to either take two shots at the end zone throwing the ball, or run one slow-developing passing play. Like the Veer offense on the whole, I thought we'd have to be "tricky" to score, so I decided on the latter.

From playing end my entire football career, plus coaching receivers in 1971, something apparent to me was that no defense can stop a crossing route if executed correctly. Against Xavier, we repeatedly ran "213 Bootleg," which featured a crossing route we usually ran perfectly, and the Musketeers indeed couldn't stop it. The play had the flanker run a curl and the tight end run straight down the field—both players positioned on the strong side of the field. In the backfield, the quarterback faked to the dive man, bellied back, and bootlegged to his right toward the strong side. On the weak side, the split end ran a crossing route toward the strong side. Finishing with eight catches for more than 100 yards for the game, the split end, Lanny Steed, had been usually wide open on that play the entire afternoon.

Calling down to McNally, I quickly decided to run the same play; however, knowing Xavier might finally decide to key on Lanny, I chose to run the play with a little twist—"213 Bootleg *Screen*"—which includes the right halfback, Terry

Gardner in this case, running a screen route to the weak side, leaving him as the lone receiver on that side of the field.

While I could literally hear inside the press box the people in the stands, who were all standing up at this point, hollering "hurry up, hurry up!" Reggie got the play off just as the game ended. Jerry ran the curl route, Tom bolted straight for the end zone, Lanny ran his crossing route, while Reggie faked to the dive man, Randy Kerr, and bootlegged off to his right. Needing 13 yards in one play for a victory, and actually maybe as many as 20 yards if you include how far behind the line of scrimmage the receiver would catch the ball, a screen pass perhaps seems foolish to run. And, maybe there's good reason why with me calling the plays that season, Marshall scored seven offensive touchdowns the *entire* year—only seven in 10 games! However, in *that* game against Xavier, "213 Bootleg Screen" worked like damn magic.

After bootlegging, Reggie turned and flipped the ball across to Terry, who had a clear path to the end zone since nearly the entire defense had shifted to the strong side. As Terry ran toward the goal line, there was a single defender who had an angle to bring him down. However, left tackle Jack Crabtree quickly took him out with a crunching block. The team that supposedly was going to need a "miracle" to win a single contest in 1971, discovered one in only its second game of the year, winning 15-13.

I quickly came out of the press box onto the field, and instantly was part of an emotionally filled moment like

I speculate few others have ever experienced in their lifetime. During the hysterical, joyous chaos, I hugged McNally, Terry Gardner, and God knows who else. I wanted to also hug the campus minister and team chaplain, Rev. Robert Scott, but he raced by me overjoyed and across the field, in his own words, "running like a fool."

The celebration in the locker room was just as emotional, especially for me when I was presented the game ball by the team. Perhaps even more moving was the sight of Donald Childers, father of the late Roger—the linebacker-turned-team manager, my "100 percenter." Donald walked around the locker room congratulating everybody, while surely his deceased son was there too in spirit. Surely, they were *all* there—somewhere in the same Fairfield Stadium locker room they had used the season before—celebrating alongside of us.

I'm not sure exactly how long the team stayed in the locker room, but it might have been as long as forty-five minutes, before we reentered the field. To our amazement, the stands remained completely filled with fans standing, celebrating, and some still crying. The surreal scene was like a repeat from four hours before—a sellout crowd cheering their Herd as we entered the stadium. Everybody wanted to remain in the moment, and no one wanted to go home.

But, eventually, we all had to go home.

During the season, and away from football, I continued on an emotional roller-coaster ride, so to speak. For one, I discovered that fall I was going to be a father for the first time—to a daughter. Adversely, during that time, I heard from a number of mothers, especially one in particular, who had stayed in touch with me since the plane crash killed their sons. Over the phone, all they wanted to do was cry and, I assumed, for me to listen. I wanted to help in any way I could, so I sat there and listened, occasionally offering whatever words of encouragement that came to mind. Perhaps only in the slightest, I think I may have helped them. I still pray today that I helped those mothers.

In football, the celebration of a victory—even the most historical and monumental—can only last a week, at most. And, such was the case following the Xavier win when we traveled to Oxford, Ohio, to face the Miami University Redskins, as they were nicknamed back then. Coached by Bill Mallory during one of his first seasons of a long, successful college head-coaching tenure lasting almost thirty years, Miami had one of the best defenses in the country, and they definitely exhibited it against us.

After we had more than 20 first downs and 350 total yards against Xavier, Marshall totaled two and two, respectively, at Miami. That's not a misprint; we had only *two* first downs and gained a grand total of just *two* yards for the entire game in a 66-6 rout. Our only touchdown came on special teams when basketball standout-turned-linebacker Dave Smith blocked a punt that Flip returned for a touchdown. It didn't help the offense that Reggie, who had injured his shoulder in practice during the week, didn't suit up. Of course, Reggie didn't play on defense, and Miami was able to move the ball even with third and fourth stringers late in the game. Suffering from a sore right upper leg,

Blake was also hurt, but had no other choice but to be our placekicker since we didn't have any others. So, and get this, he kicked left-footed—that is, with his opposite leg. The result could have actually been worse but Mallory, a class act, tried to keep from running up the score, and was embarrassed afterward that his team scored as many points. As was Jack, who made the team line up following the game and look at the scoreboard, ingraining in the players' minds the sight of a humbling defeat.

Speaking of affecting the mind, the following week we had to board a plane and fly to DeKalb, Illinois, for our game at Northern Illinois—the team's first flight in just under eleven months since the tragedy. To Jack's credit, he informed the players that any of them could skip the trip if they were apprehensive about flying, and it wouldn't jeopardize their position on the team. Although just one player didn't make the trip, everyone—players and coaches, and whether they were part of the team in 1970, or not—was at least a little nervous about flying. And, if any of them say anything different, they're damn lying. There were a lot of guys lined up, putting quarters in kiosks selling life insurance at the airport. I later heard as we walked outside to board the plane, that there in plain sight was a casket on a gurney in an open bay of the aircraft. I'm glad I didn't notice that casket, or there may have been two members of the Marshall team not making that trip.

We supposedly had no chance at Northern Illinois. They had a big-time passing offense, featuring the second-leading receiver in the nation behind, ironically, my brother

Rhett at FSU, in Willie Hatter. In just the first half, Hatter caught nearly 10 passes for more than 120 yards; however, somehow, the Huskies led by a score of only 7-6. Down 7-0 just before halftime, we surely gave Northern Illinois a scare when Flip intercepted a pass and returned it for a touchdown.

At halftime, Northern Illinois decided to drastically change its offensive game plan from mostly passing to running the ball down our throats, and it worked like a charm. Entering the fourth quarter, Marshall suddenly trailed 30-6 and to seemingly make matters worse, we had lost Reggie to another injury. Regardless, Dave stepped in and put on an unbelievable single-quarter offensive performance. For the game, he completed 10 passes for over 200 yards, threw for a touchdown, and ran for another. Lanny finished with 159 receiving yards, which was the second-most in Marshall history at the time, and 30 more than Northern Illinois' Hatter gained. The Young Thundering Herd lost 37-18, but it was considered a moral victory of sorts since it was believed we had finally discovered an offense.

Apparently, if an offense is discovered one week, it can instantly and completely disappear for the rest of the season. A second-rate team already, the Young Thundering Herd started to experience injuries that really impacted the offense. We had our moments, like Reggie and Dave combining to set a new single-game school completion record at Western Michigan; however, we curiously couldn't score in Kalamazoo, losing 37-0. In fact, we could hardly score the rest of the season, getting shut out in five of the final six games following the Northern Illinois game. There were definitely some low times during October and November of that season; plus, there was another time or two that was even lower—downright dreadful.

The weekend of the season's next-to-last game against Toledo was not only the one-year anniversary of the plane crash, but we just happened to be facing the No. 14 team in the country, who was also riding a 32-game winning streak. It was essentially the same Toledo team that had defeated us 52-3 the season before with the great Chuck Ealey at quarterback, Don Fair at receiver, a few good running backs, and All-American tackle Mel Long spearheading maybe the best defense in college football. About the only thing that had changed for the Rockets in a year was they had a new head coach after Frank Lauterbur had left for Iowa.

The morning of the game on November 13th, a private service was held by Father Scott for relatives and friends of the deceased. Just before kickoff, a wreath ceremony was conducted at the stadium by former acting president Donald Dedmon, who was serving as the university's vice president of academic affairs. Jack, the three surviving lettermen, and the three surviving coaches, including myself, placed a wreath in remembrance at the base of the scoreboard. Another wreath was placed there as well by the Toledo captains and their head coach. That was a really tough ceremony to get through and then, we somehow had to be promptly prepared to face mighty Toledo.

I'll say this about that Marshall defense—when our offense couldn't score points the last half of the season, those defenders sure didn't play like a bunch of outmanned newcomers. They had heart, were aggressive, and often kept us in ballgames into the third quarter; however, then depth and inexperience would eventually catch up as it faltered the last quarter or so. Against Toledo, the same was true. Each totaling more than 20 tackles, linemen Chuck Wright and Odell Graves were all over the Rockets' offense. Despite having a deep bruise on the back of his arm, Toledo's Ealey started but was removed for a backup after throwing a touchdown in the first quarter. The Rockets scored again in the second quarter, but led only 14-0 at halftime, and 21-0 into the fourth quarter. Then, our defense simply gave out, while Toledo's head coach decided to escalate things.

The Rockets were still throwing the football late in the game, while holding a 36-0 lead. With 30-something seconds remaining, it appeared we had forced them to punt from around our 40-yard line. Just as I was thinking about what we would run on offense after returning the punt, I noticed standing back to receive the snap wasn't Toledo's normal punter, but the backup quarterback who had played most of the game. Running a fake punt, the "punter" lofted a long pass for a touchdown, and the Rockets would win, 43-0.

I was beyond pissed! How in the hell could a head coach allow his team to run a fake punt with a 36-0 lead, and against a host which had allowed him and his players to be part of a pregame service in memory of those that had died? This same head coach would say he only started

Ealey at quarterback "because of all the emotional pressure, the memorial services and all." I raced out of the press box and onto the field to find the head coach. When I did, I put a real cussing on him, including calling him a name I won't repeat.

I guess someone eventually told on me because when I got to work the following Monday, I was informed by the same high-ranking administrator I've mentioned several times before that I was to immediately write an apology letter to Toledo's head coach, which I did. I congratulated him on the win, said it was by far the best team the Herd had played since I had coached at Marshall, admitted I had completely lost my mind, and asked him to accept my apology. Nonetheless, looking at the carbon copy of the letter I saved, it appears I didn't let him off the hook completely. Surely, I wrote, the head coach wasn't fully aware of the circumstances that day—families there for the anniversary of the tragedy, facing a young and inexperienced team—for if he had been fully aware, "you would have had second thoughts on throwing the ball and running up the score. I can understand your thoughts of maintaining or even bolstering national statistics, but I cannot rationalize for you." I then wished him the best of luck in the Tangerine Bowl.

Earlier in the season, on the day before Halloween, amidst those five games of not scoring a single point, we had a diamond in the rough, so to speak, where we scored just enough to pull off what some consider an even bigger miracle that season than defeating Xavier on the final play.

Bowling Green entered our Homecoming game in Huntington having lost only one game all year, and that was to Toledo. The Falcons were fresh off a four-touchdown win over Miami—the same team that had defeated us by 60 points. Plus, they were seeking a bowl bid, and the much inferior Young Thundering Herd seemed certain not to stand in their way. Bowling Green was probably the best team we had faced through the first seven games of the year, and undoubtedly the biggest and strongest. However, just as Kentucky demonstrated at Florida State in 1964, if a team is not prepared for the weather, a "big" team can be more sluggish than strong. With a high temperature reaching an unseasonal 80 degrees, or about 15 degrees higher than normal for that time in Huntington, and more than 20 degrees higher than it was in Bowling Green that weekend, I truly believe the Falcons had prepared for a game to be played in chilly to mild conditions.

In front of a sellout crowd, it was obvious from the start Bowling Green's offense, which had entered the game ranked near the top 10 in the nation, was rather lethargic. As the Falcons kept punting or turning the ball over, it seemed like every time I looked towards their sideline from the press box, at least one or two of them was puking, just like unprepared Kentucky had done in Tallahassee. Meanwhile on offense, we had decided during the week to switch up our game plan and utilize what we had failed to establish all season—a running game. With Bowling Green expecting the pass, we ran the ball, primarily with John Johnstonbaugh, who rushed for nearly 100 yards against an excellent defense. In the second quarter, Reggie led us on a long drive capped by a touchdown run by John. The Falcons cut their deficit to 6-3 with a field goal in the third quarter. Towards the end of the stanza, Reggie led Marshall from its own 20-yard line to the opposing 25; however, he was injured while running a keeper, and had to leave the game. In stepped Dave again.

Facing 3rd down and 5 yards to go, Dave was tackled a few yards behind the line of scrimmage while trying to find a receiver, bringing up 4th down. We were too close to Bowling Green's end zone to punt the ball, and we certainly weren't going to try a field goal, so there was only one option. On maybe our second-most critical offensive play of the season, behind only the winning touchdown pass against Xavier, Dave completed a short pass of about five yards to Lanny, who then got a few more on his own, barely picking up the first down to the 20-yard line. Six plays later—all rushes—Dave ran for a two-yard touchdown on third down, giving us a 12-3 lead.

After a long kickoff return, Bowling Green quickly scored a touchdown to pull within two points. Late in the game and still trailing 12-10, the Falcons came flying down the field passing the ball, and had a first down around our 20-yard line with a minute and a half left.

I can't say enough good things about Charles Henry—at that time, the youngest starting linebacker in all of college football at only seventeen years old. Against Bowling Green, he refused to allow injuries and lack of depth again hinder the defense down the stretch. At one point,

Charles made a tackle and hurt his leg so badly, he couldn't come off the field until it was fitted with an air cast. We all thought he had broken his leg. Nevertheless, on the next series, there goes Charles back on the field.

With plenty of time remaining and already in field goal range, Bowling Green only gained two yards in three plays against Marshall's aggressive, inspired defense led by Henry, resulting in a 37-yard field goal attempt. Seeking a one-point victory, the Falcons' kick sailed off to the right. We ran out the rest of the clock for the most unlikely of victories.

The Young Thundering Herd had accomplished for a second time what supposedly would take a "miracle" to occur just once: win a ballgame. And, although we'd finish with a 2-8 record, by all accounts and purposes it was a successful season. Many programs encountering what we had gone through would not have fielded a team that year. And, history shows if a college football team elects not to play, it will usually remain dormant.

At Marshall, it would have been easy to drop football and, if we had done so temporarily following the tragedy, I believe the university would have likely never fielded a team again. Instead, the Young Thundering Herd paid the price in defeats, while capturing a couple of miracles along the way, to lay a foundation to eventually achieve success—prosperity which seemed to be right around the corner. Home attendance had increased from averaging roughly 8,000 spectators in '70 to more than 12,000 only a year later, about 3,000 of whom were season-ticket holders—staggering numbers considering the program had nearly become obsolete *twice* within the previous few years. And, with the team returning all but a couple of starters in 1972, never before had there been a program so upbeat after winning just two games. The 1971 season was rightfully labeled "The Beginning" of Marshall football.

I, on the other hand, was, in a word, confused. I mean, I've been confused for much of my life, but I was really confused then. From me receiving the game ball after the Xavier win to celebrating after beating Bowling Green—what had to be one of the biggest upsets in college football history—to an optimistic future, I was confused the entire time. I was unable to fully relish those moments like the rest of the team, but instead questioned if I wanted to be part of it all. What was "The Beginning" for the rest of the Marshall football program was looking more like perhaps "The End" for me.

CHAPTER 9
TRYING TO SURVIVE MY GUILT

AT OUR FIRST FOOTBALL banquet since before the tragedy, the unthinkable transpired: a West Virginia University head football coach was selected as the keynote speaker for a Marshall football gala. Marshall didn't think of WVU as a rival; you actually have to play one another to constitute a rivalry. At the time, the two schools—by far, the two largest colleges in the state—had played one another in football *and* basketball only about a half-dozen times, and not since the 1920s or 1930s. The Herd was seen as the Mountaineers' inferior little brother, and treated as such. Yet although Marshall was inferior to a West Virginia program experiencing continued success and heading to a bowl game, the primary thought among many of the 350 Marshall supporters that night at the Memorial Student Center was, "I hope someone asks the WVU head coach when the two teams will finally play against one another."

Following the death of sports information director and play-by-play man Gene Morehouse in the crash, Bob Wagner became the radio voice of the Herd. Serving as master of ceremonies, Bob introduced athletic director

Joe McMullen to open the banquet. In a very serious and sincere manner, McMullen introduced the WVU head coach, thanking him for agreeing to be the speaker and helping to make the banquet "a success." What followed was the Mountaineers' head coach, my dear friend Bobby Bowden, speaking to a large contingent of Marshall fans, some of whom had not been particularly inviting. Bobby delivered a brilliant speech—an appropriate mixture of joking and sincerity—which could have captivated any audience.

In memory of the late Dave Griffith, the captain of the 1970 team, Dave's widow, Nancy, and I gave out special leadership awards. Dave left a one-year-old daughter when he died in the crash. Handing out the awards with Nancy to defensive lineman Chuck Wright and tight end Randy Kerr was an emotional, difficult thing to do. During Chuck's acceptance speech, he apologized to the crowd for "not giving Marshall a winner." Reacting to what Chuck said and addressing the audience, Bobby emphasized, "You *are* winners," regarding the Marshall football program.

For about five minutes, although it felt like an eternity, Bobby poked fun at me. He told the crowd that while we were at Florida State, he and the other coaches once asked me what my IQ was. "Red said it was '20-20,'" Bobby announced with a laugh.

Full of praise, Bobby spoke of our upset win over Bowling Green. He stated that since we obviously didn't outmuscle the big, powerful Falcons, our victory was achieved in an even better manner: we "out-spirited them."

Bobby ended the banquet by wishing Marshall well: "I hope you win them all next year," he declared, and then added, "I hope you all wish that we win at least a couple." He received a much-deserved standing ovation.

Despite what many considered the success of that season, there was a tremendous amount of recruiting to be done. In an effort to help shore up our 1972 recruiting class, I had planned a recruiting trip that would take me through the southern portion of the state. I approached the athletic office, asking for a school vehicle for the trip, but was informed, "The state's cars are currently not road worthy." So, I was told to use my personal car, and I'd get reimbursed for any travel expenses.

After the recruiting trip, I submitted my expense report to the athletic business manager. About a week and half later, I approached the manager and asked for my check. He said that although he had written it, he curiously was no longer in possession of my check. For some reason, the high-ranking administrator wanted to hold it for me.

I went to the administrator, asking for my check. He said he had it, but wanted to talk to me first. He first asked why I had taken my personal car on the recruiting trip, which I explained. I was then instructed I should always take a state vehicle if it's available. This was followed by the administrator questioning the route I took compared to the mileage I had reported. This was all bull, and only an attempt to harass me. As his voice escalated, he then said that "it was time somebody straightened" me out. I attempted to explain my mileage and route, but should have kept quiet.

The administrator inexplicably began to yell at me. I got up to leave, whereupon he ran over, grabbed my arm, and ordered me to "sit down!" I wouldn't. On his third command to "sit down," he added, "or start looking for a new job!" At that moment, I had no choice but to sit down.

The administrator began lecturing me, calling me "disloyal," bringing up the fact I didn't have a master's degree. At some point, I got up and left. I forget whether or not I even got my expense check. But, more so, this is more or less when it seems I forgot an *entire year* as it relates to Marshall University and its football program.

I cannot explain it but, as I indicated earlier, I somehow lost the 1972 football season. I can recall the most intricate details from my childhood, and I can detail football games I played and coached in according to the teams I faced, and the seasons they occurred, but I have absolutely no memory of being an assistant at Marshall in '72. But, as pointed out to me when I began this book project, I apparently did indeed coach that season.

Evidently, the label of the "Young Thundering Herd," which was supposed to be the team's nickname for four seasons, lasted for only one year when head coach Jack Lengyel changed his mind, deciding only the '71 squad would have the nickname. I also don't recall Carl Koker, one of the surviving coaches and my friend, leaving the program several months prior to the start of the 1972 season. Carl's departure, plus the addition of a new assistant, shifted the staff around to where I apparently coached defensive backs in 1972, which I cannot even remember doing.

I do recall a few sparse incidents, like definitely for two years being the position coach for Roy Tabb—the namesake of the "Roy Tabb Drill," and heavily recruiting and then signing wide receiver John "Fuzzy" Filliez, who was also being lured by the likes of Virginia Tech, Pittsburgh, and Penn State, and originally signing with West Virginia—incidents which place me at Marshall during the 1972-73 academic year. I've been informed fairly recently that Roy's second year in the program was the 1972 season, whereas Fuzzy signed with Marshall in the winter of 1973 before beginning a Thundering Herd career that ended with him ranking in the top ten in NCAA Division I history in receptions. I remember these instances, and a few others like them, but I've always associated them with the 1971-72 academic year. Also, whenever I recall getting up and leaving the high-ranking administrator's office as he yelled at me in May 1972, I've always believed I resigned from Marshall in the same office soon thereafter, and not over a year later.

I have been informed by so-called experts my repressed memories stem from the stressful and traumatic incidents I experienced. More so than anything, these experts assert, they came about as a result of the extreme survivor's guilt I endured soon after the crash.

Why do the repressed memories relate to Marshall University and its football program specifically during the 1972-73 academic year? No one seems to know the answer to that one. I wonder why the repressed memories can't be from before, like the aftermath of the plane crash. I sure in hell would prefer to forget about the tragedy instead of simply the 1972 football season.

I do recall that what I experienced as survivor's guilt really manifested itself after the 1971 season, or more than a year after the crash. The best way to describe how I experience the guilt, even currently every so often, is initially feeling a very uneasy sensation in the back of my head, like spiders, rats, or snakes crawling or gnawing at the base of my brain. When awake, the sensation leads me into deep thought and then extreme depression. When asleep, the sensation transitions into a sense of someone or something chasing me—a hellacious nightmare. Because they were rather routine at first, the nightmares started to affect my sleeping—or, lack thereof—and me physically. When Marshall's memorial fountain was dedicated in 1972 to honor those who perished in the crash, I remember two things the most. First, I weighed about 185 pounds, down from around 235 to 240 when the tragedy occurred. Secondly, this was my first and final appearance for a long, long time in public view at the annual ceremony before I started hiding behind the sycamore tree.

That summer, although as indicated, I always thought it occurred the summer before, I decided I didn't want to coach anymore. Although my desire to leave Marshall was primarily due to the tragedy constantly being on my mind, I was also burned out with coaching, and frustrated with certain school administrators. But more so, I was upset with myself because of my mental condition. The only thing I believed I could do to no longer be upset with administrators and not to be burned out, plus hoping it would help relieve my survivor's guilt, was to quit Marshall, which I decided to do. I had wanted to be the next great football coach, but it looked like I was going to have to head in a different direction.

When I informed the high-ranking administrator of my decision in his office, how odd it was when he jumped out of his chair in absolute anger, breathing heavily like a picadored bull. He was *so* mad, I fully expected steam to come spewing out of his ears like in the cartoons. But, I was pretty sure he wasn't upset because I was leaving Marshall, but frustrated I was leaving on my own terms, and not when he had intended. He started to put his hands on me, when I backed away and said, "Wait just a second (his first name), I don't work for you anymore. Don't do something you'll be sorry for." In other words, take your hands off me or I'll kick your ass and, unlike before, I don't care if I lose this job.

I had a new job. I had been in contact with a friend who owned a construction company in the Huntington area. I took a job with his company as a "management trainee," where I was to train in the field for some time until I became familiar with everything, before eventually coming into the office to work in management—though the latter never occurred. I discovered "management trainee" was a term to help the ego of a college graduate, who was more like a "shovel man." I was paid $7.00 per hour and $40 per month for insurance. I had no retirement, sick leave, or vacation and, on Saturdays, worked the first half of the day. Any errands I had to run for the week were done during the last half of the day. I earned around $14,500 my first year, but was told it would increase to about $18,000 to $20,000 my second year—though the latter didn't occur either. Still, my first-year pay was about 50 percent more than what I made as a football coach. However, I was away from my family about three-fourths of the time, living in dirty construction trailers. Although I was usually away from home, looking back, working for the construction company was exactly what I needed at the time. I needed someone to tell me every move I was to make. More than anything, I needed to work *hard*. I found the harder I worked, the easier I was able to sleep at night without experiencing nightmares.

I remember vividly laying in my bunk bed about 150 miles from home in Ronceverte, West Virginia. It had rained for a couple of days, and rain usually meant we couldn't work. This meant there was a good chance I would encounter another restless, nightmare-filled night. Laying inside the construction trailer, I had woken up in a cold sweat after another unbelievably crazy, yet seemingly very realistic, recurring nightmare. And, to avoid re-visiting the nightmare, I was damn sure not going to try to go back to sleep. So, I just laid there, waiting for a new day to begin, and praying it would be dry enough to where I could work—*hard* work.

To this day, I have no idea what triggers the nightmares. For the longest time, I believed talking about the tragedy likely triggered them. So, I avoided talking about the plane crash, my friends who perished, and everything else concerning the tragedy. But, I continued to have the nightmares. Whatever brought them on—the devil, perhaps—they were damn scary. Normally, I wake up unable to give details regarding who or what had been after me, or shooting at me. However, when I can recollect, like that night in Ronceverte, it's always the same two people pursuing me: oddly, Captain Frank Abbott and Charlene Poat.

I never met Captain Abbott, the pilot of the crashed airplane, or Ms. Poat, one of the two stewardesses on the flight—never knew who they were and never even caught a glimpse of either of them prior to the crash. The only thing I can think is I must have seen their photos in a newspaper following the crash. I associated the two faces in my nightmares as Abbott and Poat and, as I've discovered in photos over the years, the pair appears identical to how they looked in real life. I don't know how they got in my head, but they did—unmistakable faces with distinct features—haunting me, coming after me.

Looking back on it, I needed professional help, and as soon as possible. However, as far as getting counseling, or seeing a psychologist or psychiatrist, this was the early 1970s, and it simply wasn't an option for me. Back then, I felt "real" men, "macho" men, didn't need counseling.

Although counseling was not an option, I had bought a book, and was nearly ashamed in doing so, to hopefully help me cope with my problems: *I'm OK—You're OK*, a self-help book about how you're supposed to think. In addition, I had gotten a book on Psycho-Cybernetics—how your mind should work like a guided missile system, guiding you to success. Lying in my bunk bed, I decided that obviously my mind was not "right," and I began reading the self-help book. I would eventually read both books, and a few others, but they didn't seem to do much for me. I discovered there was only one thing that helped me cope, namely, hard work, but it wasn't going to happen as long as it was raining.

In 1974, my anger and frustration escalated with the passing of my father. He died from complications of PSP, or progressive supra nuclear palsy—a rare degenerate disease involving the deterioration of the brain. Actor Dudley Moore would later die from the same thing. It has never escaped me how determined my father was for his three sons to become "real" men, so much so that when I was younger, he believed I couldn't hit, or punch adequately. So, he made me practice punching by boxing my younger sister. I'm not sure if boxing my sister helped, but I feel satisfied my father—ironically, a man with a Napoleon complex, who stood at five-foot-seven, or eight inches shorter than me—passed away believing he had made a man out of me.

At this time, my ever-increasing anger, frustration, shame, guilt, and you could have probably thrown in a few others, was mostly directed at Marshall and its football program. I didn't want to be around it in the least bit, and avoided it at all costs. Perhaps above all, I didn't want to be around the program because I felt like others would think I was interfering. I avoided the sport of football altogether, to where I even refused to watch it on television. However, it would soon become evident it was going to be difficult for me to totally disassociate myself from Marshall football and the rebuilding of its program.

Following a record of 9-33 during the 1971 to 1974 seasons, Jack resigned as Marshall's head football coach. He then went into the wholesale furniture business for a few years before returning to college athletics in 1978 as the associate athletic director of the University of Louisville. This began a hell of a collegiate athletics administration career for him in which he served six different major universities—an administrative career lasting for nearly thirty years, during which time he primarily served as an athletic director. In September of 1978, a local writer wrote a piece about Jack returning to college athletics. Recounted was Jack's arrival at Marshall following the tragedy and him encountering "one leftover aide, miffed at not being chosen for the top job, [who] turned into kind of a departmental 'mole.'" Jack would have had better success at Marshall but, "the mole proved to be a minor problem."

I knew the writer was speaking of me, as did several people who phoned my house, questioning the article. In fact, most people who knew about Marshall football and its rebuilding stage could recognize the writer was talking about me. I was beyond pissed off. I had been misquoted in newspapers before, but never associated with something which was absolutely not true. Although I had mixed emotions from time to time, I had given 100 percent to Marshall football, including as an assistant under Jack, recruiting hard until the very end. Yet, I was regarded as being a "mole" at that time—"a problem."

My knee-jerk reaction was to promptly call Jack, who I hadn't spoken to since I had been an assistant under him. I was to the point, asking him if he had told the sportswriter—did he really think—I had been some sort of problem. "I never said that," was Jack's response.

After five or six years in construction, I had worked my way up to a field superintendant, and thought I was doing a pretty good job. One day, I made some suggestions to the owner about some manhole covers to do a particular job more efficiently. The owner paused—almost taken aback—and responded with "that's just not the way we do it here." I said I was just trying to help. "Well, Red, if you think it ought to be done a certain way, maybe you should start your own business." The owner started laughing, as did the rest of the guys on the site. I was a little ticked off, but it must have motivated me. Soon afterward, I took his advice, and indeed started my own construction business.

Running my own business, I soon discovered I was a pretty good coach—"coaching" construction. Just as Ray Eliot's "football philosophy" claims, everything starts in one's mind. I learned to motivate my employees by first connecting with their approach to working. I would start their day by informing them, for example, all we had to do was install 200 more feet of pipe, backfill it, and do it correctly, and we'd then quit for the day. But, they'd get credited for eight hours of work. Well, hell, I had never seen such a motivated group. So, I ran with the approach.

By 1978, although I was still having the occasional nightmare, and I remained mad at everything related to Marshall, overall, I was finally feeling okay. I enjoyed my work, and enjoyed its 12-hour days—hard-working days that usually put me fast asleep.

After one of those hard-working days one Saturday evening in mid-November, I walked into our family room and noticed the television had been left on. Just as I reached to flip the switch off, I spotted a familiar, friendly, and reassuring face on the screen—that of Bobby Bowden. After six seasons as West Virginia's head coach, Bobby was in his third year at Florida State, and the Seminoles were hosting Navy on ABC-TV back when FSU football was broadcast on TV only about once or twice a year. And, here I just happened upon the game. I hadn't witnessed football since the last game I coached about six years before, but decided that maybe I'd watch a few minutes only to see if they'd show Bobby again. As it turned out, a few minutes wound up being the entire game—a win for the Seminoles.

While at Florida State, Bobby would become synonymous with winning on the field, while having the ability to captivate an audience off of it. I can also add that he is such a presence in people's lives, he actually captivated me through a television screen, and got me back in touch with something I once loved but had avoided for the longest time—football.

CHAPTER 10
FINALLY, A PART OF "WE"

"TAILGATING—WHAT THE HELL IS that?" I asked my good friend Joe Feaganes sometime during the late 1980s, having never heard of the expression.

"It's when fans party before and after a football game," replied Joe, Marshall's accomplished head golf coach. "They eat and drink in a grass parking lot."

Joe must have noticed a look of skepticism on my face, adding, "Don't worry, you don't have to watch the game—just tailgate."

After Marshall won the fewest games in all of major college football during the decade of the 1970s—only 22—the 1980s began almost as badly. However, with the Herd competing at the I-AA level by the middle of the decade, what once seemed improbable actually transpired: Marshall became a winner. In 1984, head coach Stan Parrish led the Thundering Herd to their first winning season in 20 years. Just three years after that, George Chaump coached Marshall to a berth in the I-AA national championship game.

Although following from afar through the newspapers, I kept my distance from the school and its football program

I still somewhat resented. One of the last things I wanted to do was associate myself again with Marshall by watching a football game at Fairfield Stadium, and Joe knew this. However, I guessed it wouldn't hurt anything for me to party outside the stadium. So, I started to "just tailgate" for Marshall games.

Soon after he became the new head coach of the Herd in 1990, I got a message that Jim Donnan wanted to speak with me. I knew of Jim as a standout quarterback for NC State while in college, a young assistant at my alma mater, Florida State, in the early 1970s, and the offensive coordinator of the great Oklahoma wishbone teams of the mid-to-late 1980s, but nothing more. I was surprised Jim invited me to attend practice one day. I turned him down. He called a couple of other times, inviting me to various things, and I just made an excuse each time why I couldn't attend. But, I would eventually run out of excuses.

During the 1990 season, the late Ted Shoebridge was being inducted into the Marshall Hall of Fame, which happened to coincide with Jim speaking at a touchdown club meeting. In a similar manner to almost twenty years before, when Teddy's mother, Yolanda, asked me to take her out to the crash site, I got word she and her husband, Ted Sr., wanted to see me again. Another invite from Jim, a drive with the Shoebridges from the airport, a hall of fame induction ceremony, and a touchdown club meeting later, I was instantly associated with the Marshall football program again after almost two whole decades trying to avoid it like the plague.

During one tailgate around the time Jim coached Marshall to a national championship in 1992, I felt "insulated" by a few beers before the game, and someone actually talked me into entering the stadium—the newly built Marshall University Stadium (now the Joan C. Edwards Stadium). However, I didn't last too long inside. In the stadium, I soon felt the "gnawing" of the rats, spiders, and snakes in the back of my head, and had to immediately leave—too much guilt and shame, I guess.

When Jim departed for the University of Georgia in 1996, Bobby Pruett stepped in as the Herd's head coach. Bobby had played football at Marshall, ironically playing on the 1964 team, along with Mickey Jackson, which had been the last winning squad at the school prior to the '84 team. Having been the defensive coordinator at Florida under Steve Spurrier, Bobby picked up exactly where Jim had left off as far as success on the gridiron and, personally, made me feel welcomed and comfortable again around the program. Bobby is undoubtedly a "personality" guy, and it was difficult to say no to him when he asked me to associate with the team.

In Bobby's first season, Marshall won all 15 of their games en route to its second I-AA national championship. Remarkably, the season marked the Herd's sixth national title appearance in the previous ten years after the program had nearly been forced to disband on two separate occasions twenty-five to thirty years before. It was then time for Marshall to play "big-boy football," and return to the conference that had almost forced our hand to drop the sport decades before.

Two-and-a-half years after getting booted out of the Mid-American Conference, Marshall filed for readmission in January 1972. Some people associated with the school really hoped for acceptance, like athletic director Joe McMullen, who was regarded as "MACMullen" by some for his desire to reunite with the conference. And, then there were those who did not—those who felt our exile from the MAC had been a slap in the face—like many students, who wore sweatshirts declaring "MAC SUCKS" (a controversial statement to print on a shirt back then). Nevertheless, having been denied readmission in 1972, after twenty-five years Marshall resumed its affiliation with the conference to compete on the I-A level.

In addition to all the success the program had experienced the previous decade, plus moving up to I-A, and featuring probably the best receiver in college football, Randy Moss, Marshall football started to draw a lot of national attention.

Growing up in Rand, a small town in West Virginia of around 1,500 residents situated near Huntington, the lanky, six-foot-four Moss was considered to be maybe the most athletic wide receiver in the history of high school football. Although Moss eventually signed to attend school and play football at then-I-AA Marshall, he had arrived back home to Huntington in a rather roundabout way. Notre Dame dismissed Moss for a fight he was involved in while in high school, followed by Florida State's dismissal for failing a drug test. However, Coach Pruett decided to give him another chance at college football.

While at Marshall, Moss was, and still is the finest athlete I have ever seen in my life. For what it's worth, the future college and Pro Football Hall-of-Famer ranks just above Florida State's Deion Sanders as far as players I have seen live possessing the most athleticism. The late Joe Hood, our star halfback at Marshall from 1969-1970, is a close third. When Moss arrived at Marshall, he brought with his athleticism also a lot of baggage. He had a mouth on him that could get him into trouble, like when he once indicated to the media the plane crash was "nothing big" to him. Plus, his cornrow-wearing, rap-music-listening representation of a so-called "thug" made him stick out like a sore thumb in the Bible-Rust-Coal Belt community.

During the 1997 football season, the media, namely *Sports Illustrated* and *TIME*, did feature stories on Marshall, essentially chronicling the same things: the program's recent success after decades of lowly play, and Moss. And, for me at the time, with that attention came the media's desire to also examine the plane crash. I was interviewed by the two magazines and asked generally the same questions about the tragedy and, curiously, Moss, giving each writer more or less the same answers. Regardless, I would feel totally different about the two pieces upon their releases: I really enjoyed one article, and thought it was fairly written; whereas, I felt at the time, the other article portrayed Moss in a bad light.

I was fortunate to have gotten to know Randy a little and thought people should give him a break before judging him. When he said the plane crash was "nothing big," I was convinced he didn't know the extent of what he was saying. And, when I was asked about Moss's brushes with the law, including the fight in high school, which was in support of a friend, and his cornrows and rap music, I told them a story about a guy I knew at Florida State. This guy played football and wasn't necessarily known for fighting to help a friend but rather for fighting his own teammates for playing time. Like Moss, this same guy also wore an unconventional haircut—a close buzz cut, nearly skin-headed—and listened to music by a singer not really mainstream at the time—Hank Williams Sr., or Luke the Drifter. Therefore, I informed some in the media, while at Florida State, I too had been called a "thug," and so maybe I had seen a little bit of my old self in Randy Moss. Of course, I added, he was a "little bit" of a better receiver than I had been.

Marshall opened its 1997 season on the road at West Virginia—the first time the two schools had faced off in football in seventy-four years. And, I was the Thundering Herd and Coach Pruett's guest on the sidelines as an honorary coach. What an honor! I had a great time, especially since we nearly upset the Mountaineers. Never did I think I would be yelling along the Marshall sidelines again. I had come a long way since a few short years before when I had to leave the stadium because of the "gnawing" in the back of my head. Sure, there was the occasional disturbing flashback or memory during the game, but at least the gnawing had gone away—for now.

After the 42-31 loss to West Virginia, where we actually led 31-28 heading into the final quarter, Bobby jokingly informed the media that the Thundering Herd had done just fine while he was coaching. It wasn't until he allowed his honorary coach to take over in the fourth quarter that Marshall surrendered its lead to the Mountaineers and lost the game. I may have "lost" the game for the team but, thanks to Bobby, I gained total reunification with the Marshall football program.

A year or two later, my wife and I decided to move to another house in Huntington. While packing some boxes, I came across my game ball from the 1971 Xavier game—which my daughter had decorated years before with stick-em-like tape detailing the victory. The more I thought about it, the more I believed the ball deserved to be somewhere else than with me. So, I soon went to the Marshall football offices, and gave my game ball to Coach Pruett, donating it to the program. As Bobby locked the ball in a trophy case, I mentioned one stipulation: if Marshall decides it has no more use for the game ball at any point in the future, that's fine, but I would then like it returned to me.

The Thundering Herd, the one-time perennial loser, remarkably was college football's most winningest program of the 1990s (114 victories). And, like the magazine articles written a few years before, the plane crash was recounted in some documentaries produced corresponding to the program's newly found success. For me personally, although I had reunited with Marshall, I wanted nothing to do with remembering the tragedy for any kind of movie. I received several phone calls over the span of about a decade, indicating they were hoping to make a movie about the plane crash, and wondering if I would be of some assistance. I politely turned down each and every one, mentioning they wouldn't be interested in the nightmares I had because of the tragedy, and Marshall University would be better suited to assist them. However, for a few video productions, and documentaries, released during that time, I did decide to take part, but only under certain conditions.

Before an interview I did with ESPN, I was very frank with their production crew. I informed them that I could get quite emotional when discussing the plane crash, its aftermath, the people involved, etc. And, if I did indeed get emotional, I didn't want to be filmed because, I thought to myself, I'm still a tough son of a gun. If I'm going to come off as anything, it's as a tough guy, not a crybaby. Sure enough, during filming, I got really emotional, wincing as I felt my eyes begin to tear up. When I opened my eyes, I saw the red light of the camera staring right at me, indicating the camera was still filming.

"Shut that damn camera off!" I shouted.

Seemingly as the entire production crew looked around to see what the hell was going on, the red light quickly went off, and my interview was over.

Several years later, I got another call asking for my assistance with a movie about the tragedy, but this request was a little different than the ones before. Instead of a would-be producer calling me, it was Keith Spears, Marshall's vice president for communications and marketing.

Keith was upfront, indicating after turning down about a dozen inadequate movie producers since he had taken office about eight years before, he had recently gotten a call from one that seemed absolutely sincere about the project. This time, Keith stressed, the producer was from Warner Bros., and a script had already been written. However, just like the others, the movie wanted me to be involved in production. Once again, I politely declined.

In late summer of 2005, on the third phone call by Keith about the possibility of a Marshall football movie, he mentioned that the producer, Basil Iwanyk, and the screenwriter, Jamie Linden, had traveled to Huntington from California to discuss the project.

"Red, you should really come. They're going to take us out for steaks [at Bobby Pruett's Steak House]," Keith said.

"Keith, I can eat a steak here at the house," I responded.

Keith indicated Warner Bros. was likely going to make a movie about the tragedy with or without Marshall's consent. However, we could assist production by advising them on sensitive portions of the story. Plus, Keith added, "Besides steak, they'll buy all the beer you can drink." They had me.

When I got to the steakhouse and saw Jamie and Basil, I didn't think the movie had a damn prayer to get off the ground. Both guys looked to be in their twenties (turns out, Jamie was about twenty-five; Basil was ten years older). Hell, I had kids older than they were, and they certainly didn't appear like they could write and produce a major motion picture. Shows you what I knew about the movie business. Jamie had gone to Florida State, so I liked him already. After talking about Seminoles football for a little bit, the next thing I knew, we were discussing the making of a movie about Marshall football. While an undergraduate at FSU, Jamie had read in the school newspaper about the tragedy on its 30th anniversary, inspiring him to write the movie script at the young age of about twenty years old. By the end of our dinner meeting, I was thoroughly impressed with Jamie and Basil. However, while speaking to them that night, the gnawing in the back of my head had returned.

At the time the movie was in pre-production, there were probably only a dozen people who knew I had coached at Marshall. That's the way I had wanted it. But I soon realized that a movie about the tragedy, where a Hollywood actor would portray me, would change all that. I was convinced that a movie where I was to serve as a so-called "consultant" would be just another reminder of the tragedy, and probably increase my nightmares—really stir the demons up after they had died down in recent years. So, if I really had no choice but to get involved in the movie, I was going to make every effort to "consult" when I could for the sake of those who perished in the tragedy—to honor them.

In mid-October of 2005, my good buddy, Ned Jones, and I were engaged in our every-other-year ritual of driving the roughly 300 miles east from Huntington to Charlottesville, Virginia, to witness Florida State play football at Virginia. A little ways into the trip, I decided to do something I had been reluctant to do: read the movie's script given to me by Jamie and Basil. After reading only a few pages, "Ugh!" I exclaimed in distaste, literally tossing the script over my shoulder and into the back seat. The script was going to have to wait; there was no use getting the trip started off on a bad foot.

Although I don't think Warner Bros. really needed my approval of the script, they asked for it. And, despite being very reluctant to read something I thought would stir up my nightmares, I eventually got around to reading the script about three weeks later. Granted, the story certainly contained some "Hollywood Fluff," or additions to the script to make the story a better movie, but it was fairly accurate and, most importantly, I believed a quality, positive piece, paying tribute to those who died in the tragedy. I, along with others at Marshall who were given an early script to read, were informed by Jamie and Basil that they would make any changes we felt were necessary. I had a few suggestions, which indeed were eventually honored. But, more so than changes needing to be made, the Marshall administration and I stressed above all to Warner Bros. that the movie had to be conscious of the families of the victims.

In time, a list of well-known actors were cast for what was to be titled *We Are Marshall*: Matthew McConaughey, who had recently been named the "Sexiest Man Alive" by *People*, as Jack Lengyel, which is ironic in itself (if you've ever seen Jack); Anthony Mackie as Nate Ruffin; Robert Patrick as Rick Tolley; David Straitham as Dr. Donald Dedmon; January Jones as my wife, Carole; and Matthew Fox as me. And, directing the movie was a guy, McGinty Nichol, who went simply by the nickname, McG.

A few weeks prior to the start of production, McG traveled to Huntington and attempted to immerse himself in the community, but discovered I wasn't the only one from the area skeptical of a movie recounting such a heartbreaking tragedy. Like me, there were those from Marshall and Huntington who were also skeptical. However, McG and the rest of the cast and crew would do a tremendous job engaging with the community, from appearing at Marshall basketball games and spring football practice to asking residents to become involved in the film by appearing as extras. Even more so, they did a great job of relaying that *We Are Marshall* would mainly be factual, honoring the victims and survivors of the tragedy, rendering respect to the Huntington community while protecting the integrity and reputation of Marshall University.

In February, I got a call from Matthew Fox, who wanted to get to know me—to study me—for several days before filming was to begin in a couple of months. There was one issue: he was filming *Lost* in Hawaii and couldn't leave the area. I would have to fly out to Honolulu for us to get to know one another. Now, as I've mentioned, although I don't enjoy flying, I'm certainly not afraid of it. However, a ten-hour flight was something else, so I hesitated. Fox emphasized it would all be paid for by Warner Bros.: the first-class flight, my stay in a downtown hotel, and all the beer I could drink on the flight (which showed that Fox had already begun to research me). Ultimately, of course, I got to hang out with Matthew Fox. Tough job.

Fox was a really great guy. From the first time he picked me up at my hotel, we seemed to really get along. Believe it or not, we had a lot in common: we were both outdoors enthusiasts who enjoyed fly fishing, and both of us had been college football receivers. He had played for three seasons while attending Columbia University in the mid-to-late 1980s.

Our days consisted of going to the filming location of *Lost* in the mornings, where we stayed for about two or three hours, followed by lunch on the set. We'd then spend the majority of the afternoons riding around together as he asked me questions. That first day, he pulled into the first convenience store he spotted, got out and said, "I have to go get something. I'll be right back." When Matthew came out, he was carrying a six-pack of beer, a can of Copenhagen, and two cups—one for each of us to spit in. Here, I would have done just about anything to quit the nasty habit of dipping, whereas he was just starting it to play me in a movie. On that first day, it was difficult for me to discuss the plane crash with Matthew, but it got a little easier as my stay wore on. In the evenings, his lovely wife, Margherita, would prepare a home-cooked meal, and along with them and their two wonderful children, Kyle and Byron, I felt like part of the family.

In April, filming began in Huntington and, although most of the reluctance from the city and Marshall had dissipated, a challenge to the movie was issued. Only identified as "A 1971 Graduate of Marshall University," someone left a three-page, handwritten note on a counter at the hotel the cast and crew were staying. Soon, the letter was photocopied, and numerous copies were passed out. The letter began, "Welcome to our little town!" and then asserted how the cast and crew was "responsible for telling the world" about he and his seventy-four "Family" members—the seventy-five people who perished in the plane crash. A segment of the letter:

> *My [Family's] story will not be an easy one to tell. I charge everyone involved to put their very soul into this challenge. We have already made the greatest of sacrifices. Make your audience feel the grief as funeral procession after procession winds down 5th Avenue and past the very buildings we gave our lives for. Translate for our audience how it feels for young men to lose game after game on the gridiron. Capture the determination on men's and women's faces as they refuse to let a team and a town die. . . . My Family and I may be gone from this earth, but we represent the hope of every son and daughter of Marshall University, and like hope, our spirit will never die. "WE ARE MARSHALL!"*

I EVENTUALLY GOT A copy of the inspiring letter. In the spring of 2006, the letter challenged me to never again stray from being a part of "We Are Marshall"—the Thundering Herd's rallying cry which began during the 1980s by fans at Fairfield Stadium. By then, I was finally and fully a part of that "We" after years of frustration, anger, and reluctance that kept me removed. Today, I always know where the letter is just in case I ever need to be reminded how important the seventy-five lives, Huntington, and Marshall University are to a lot of people.

For the football field scenes, a second stage of filming was at Morris Brown College's Herndon Stadium in Atlanta, Georgia. As a consultant, I basically just hung out around the sets. I also had a small, non-speaking role as Morehead State's head coach, where I was instructed to "just look serious." As filming progressed, I realized that Marshall University and even I, to a certain extent, would receive some national attention. But, holy moley, I was absolutely clueless to what extent the attention would be.

My consulting contract called for me to do some public relations work so, whenever I was asked to be interviewed, I obliged—over and over and over. For about thirty-five years, I pretty much could not, and refused, to talk about the tragedy. But, suddenly, I was talking about it several times a day. At first, my interviews were shaky while having a hard time controlling my emotions, but I tried to remember I was representing Marshall, and to conduct myself so I wouldn't embarrass the school and it would be proud of me. Like in Hawaii when speaking with Matthew about the tragedy, I found speaking with the media a little easier the more I did it.

Experiencing my "fifteen minutes of fame," I was regularly pictured in newspapers, seen on TV, receiving letters from people all over, and was eventually asked to give speeches. Once during filming in Atlanta, I was even approached by a lady admirer, who gave me a photo of herself with her contact information on the back. She told me that I was good looking, and asked me to come by her house. Being upfront and honest with the woman, I asked her, "Who you think you're kiddin'?" I can't make this stuff up—my brief time as a Hollywood heartthrob.

The day before *We Are Marshall* premiered in Huntington, my request to watch the movie by myself so I could be better prepared to watch it publicly the following night was fulfilled by Warner Bros. A female assistant producer watched it with me and, although someone later said she was only present just on the off chance I attempted to steal the movie and release it publicly, she kind of acted as an emotional support of sorts. While watching the movie, I was simply awful—crying, sobbing, and almost whining—so bad, I told her I needed to watch it again the next morning to be ready by the premiere. My second viewing the following morning went a little better than before. Afterwards, I asked her, "How'd I do?" She replied, "At least you didn't make those loud noises this time."

For the premiere at the Keith Albee—a historical theater in downtown Huntington—Fox and McConaughey were introducing the film on stage while I sat with Margherita and my date, Rosie. Although I had struck out seeing Rosie following the 1962 Florida State-Georgia game, I later—*much* later—became reacquainted with her after my divorce from Carole. As the lights dimmed, Fox came off the stage and joined us at the table.

"You doing okay?" he asked me.

"I think so," I replied.

"Well, this might help you during the movie," he said as he pulled two bottles of beer from his coat pocket—one for me, one for him.

"When you're done with the beer, don't throw the bottle away," he said. "We're going to need it to spit in; I couldn't find any cups," he added as he pulled out a can of Copenhagen.

Shortly thereafter, the movie opened in Hollywood. My time there was unlike anything I've ever experienced before. I think my picture was taken more in a span of five minutes than the total number of times ever before and since. Matthew Fox was just as nice and accommodating to me and Rosie in Hollywood as he was in Huntington. He accompanied me at the premiere as what seemed like thousands of flashbulbs were going off. I still joke with Rosie, telling her that what keeps our relationship going, and how she continues to put up with me, is that I am still the only person to ever get her into Hollywood.

Much more meaningful than *We Are Marshall* bringing attention to any one individual associated with Huntington or the university was how the movie inspired a rebirth, of sorts, to the local area. For example, production for the movie virtually rebuilt a portion of what had been regarded as a "ghost town"—downtown Huntington. Also, it undoubtedly played a part in the increase of Marshall's student enrollment: after roughly 1,400 incoming freshmen enrolled at the school for the academic year just prior to the movie's production, more than 2,000 entered the university just six years later in 2011. And, if there was never a movie about the plane crash, there likely would be no state historical marker at the crash site. Before the marker was erected, which occurred the day before the movie opened in Huntington, there was nothing distinguishing the crash site along West Virginia Route 75 in Wayne County except a burned hillside. The charred ground had been the site's only indicator the two times I showed the late Mrs. Shoebridge (who died in 1999) where her Teddy had perished. Now, because of *We Are Marshall*, there are road signs directing visitors to the site, where a flagpole stands, along with an observation deck which, the last time I visited, displayed a white sign proclaiming, "Never Forget—75."

We Are Marshall also tells a story—one not easy to tell—in the form of a quality film that is sensitive to the emotion-filled tragedy. The movie certainly met the challenge put forth by "A 1971 Graduate of Marshall University," and then some, strengthening the spirit of the seventy-five-member "Family," which will never die nor be forgotten.

We are Marshall!

CHAPTER 11
A SECOND CHANCE

FOR THE DURATION OF the production and showing of *We Are Marshall*, the 1970 and 1971 teams were really thrust into the spotlight. The attention generated some real heart-felt discoveries: people realizing they were connected to someone in the tragedy, whereas before, they were totally unaware of such.

One of my favorite discoveries regarded a woman, Kathy, who, as a student at Marshall thirty-six years before, had somehow come into possession of a No. 82 football practice jersey. She didn't know how she got it, or whose jersey it had been, but she had kept it safe in a dresser for decades. During all the publicity on the movie, Kathy discovered that Jack Repasy had worn No. 82. Jack was our fine receiver from Cincinnati who was part of the outstanding freshman class of 1968, before he died in the tragedy. Kathy later noticed Jack's mother, Mary Beth Repasy, quoted in a story about the movie in a Cincinnati newspaper. She contacted Mary Beth and eventually delivered the jersey to her. Kathy said, "I have come to the conclusion that I had ended up with the jersey so I could keep it safe for thirty-six years, and then return it to where it actually belongs."

Similarly, I came to the conclusion that although I had ended up with the game ball from the win over Xavier in 1971 (that ball could have gone to any number of players or coaches; all I did was call the winning play), I rightfully returned it to where it actually belonged—the Marshall University football program.

For almost a decade, the ball sat in a trophy case where the football offices were located on campus. During and soon following all the publicity surrounding the movie, there were a lot of people—many more than before—coming and going around the program: more visitors, more former players and coaches returning, more media—simply, more people who wanted to experience the football program that had been dramatized and celebrated in *We Are Marshall*. Personally, before the movie, I had never been asked by friends and family for any kind of tour of the campus and the Thundering Herd's football facilities. But that all would change around 2006, when I began taking people on a number of outings to Marshall, and always included on the tour was a stop at the trophy case containing the game ball.

One day I was showing a friend around and we stopped at the trophy case. Just as I was beginning to describe the purpose of the football behind the glass, I realized it was no longer there. I questioned the secretary about the whereabouts of the ball. I asked the guy who was in charge of maintaining memorabilia for the trophy case. I eventually even asked the athletic director if he knew what happened to it. Although absolutely familiar with the football that had stayed locked in the trophy case, nobody had a clue as to where or why it had disappeared. It was like the Xavier game ball had vanished into thin air.

I dreamt death came the other night
And Heaven's gate swung wide.

With kindly grace, an angel ushered me inside.

And there! To my astonishment
Stood folks I'd known on earth

Some I judged and labeled "unfit" and "of little worth".

Angry words rose to my lips
But never were set free,
For every face showed stunned surprise –
No one expected me!

Surprise in Heaven, by someone anonymous, which I have edited here based on how my mother used to recite it, is a poem I will remind myself of, like the afternoon at the trophy case when I discovered the Xavier game ball had been removed, whenever I'm about to unrightfully pass judgment. As it is said, "Judge not, and you will not be judged." I was "judged" for a long time, and I didn't like it. And, for a lot of my life, I may have prejudged others, but now I try to avoid doing so. Therefore, for certain circumstances, like when I believed the game ball was stolen, and suddenly names of people began to pop into my head of those who could have been the culprit, I remind myself to "judge not," for it can negatively affect the coping mechanism of an already fragile mind.

There's no doubt *We Are Marshall* accomplished a lot of good for a lot of people, the university, and the Huntington area. As indicated, for me the movie and interviews compelled me to talk about the tragedy when I had hardly done so before, even with my wife at the time. However, there comes a time when a person can only talk so much. At some point, it seemed like every time I turned around there was a camera in my face or my phone was ringing several times a day requesting an interview. I got tired of all the attention, and decided to finally get away from it for some time, in 2007. So, I drove up to a little hunting cabin I own three-and-a-half hours away to stay for a while.

Totally unexpectedly during my first night at the cabin, I had one of my damn nightmares—my first one in at least a year.

As I sat up in my bed covered in sweat, saying aloud, "I thought those horrific things might be over!" I thought of Keith Morehouse, Marshall's radio play-by-play man. I remember Keith up in Fairfield Stadium's press box when I coached; he was a kid, and his father, Gene, was the play-by-play man. Gene died in the plane crash. Keith would marry Debbie Hagley, whose parents, Dr. Ray and Shirley Hagley, had been my friends and also died in the crash.

During its publicity, the movie was regarded by some people as a memorial or a tribute to the university and how the community recovered—a kind of closure. Keith indicated that if "closure" from the tragedy was realized through the movie and all the attention resulting from it, that was certainly okay for some. "I just don't feel, for me, that that's a word that I particularly would apply," Keith said of the term "closure."

I realized that although talking about the tragedy helped repair what was going on in my head, it hadn't completely healed the damage I endured, nor would it. In a bed in a construction trailer in Ronceveret, West Virginia, I had come to the realization that my mind was not "right." About thirty-five years later, in a bed in a hunting cabin in Snowshoe, West Virginia, I discovered that besides talking about the tragedy, I needed to think differently, as well, to get my mind even more "right." I recalled that some of the parents of the players who died in the crash would continue to live and breathe their son's death. They couldn't get away from constant, tragic thoughts, and they went through absolute hell for the rest of their lives.

I concluded that in order to avoid encounters with Captain Frank Abbott and Charlene Poat, I needed to turn negative thoughts into the positive, not prejudge people, stop being mad and frustrated while holding grudges, and remember the people in the tragedy for the good they did and not for the sheer fact I would not see them again after Gail Parker and I left the East Carolina visitor's dressing room on November 14, 1970. When I close my eyes and think of, for example, the boys from Tuscaloosa we signed in 1968 and 1969, instead of thinking what a tragic, big loss it was for them to die, I try to think instead of the tremendous, big smile Robert Van Horn always had on his face. I remember sitting in the press box in Lexington and just after Kentucky's Charley Bradshaw had claimed what a tremendous group of freshmen he had, one of little Marshall's freshmen, defensive back Larry Sanders, came out of nowhere with great speed, closing the gap on a Wildcat receiver to save a touchdown as part of a historical upset. I recall Freddy Wilson who, after we moved him to tight end, would block down and cave in a whole side of a defensive line. Freddy's blocking would often spring loose his buddy, Joe Hood, who could work his magic in the open field. Joe had a quick, subtle move that could make a defender literally fall on his ass as if he had been shot from the press box. These were just four of the more than thirty players on the plane, many of whom were great athletes, but even more of them were great human beings of high character and integrity.

In continuing to heal, while I try to remember the good in the people I knew in the tragedy, I try hard to believe, as Oscar Wilde said, there's always something good in *everyone*. But, admittedly, sometimes I have to try *really* hard to believe that.

A year or two before Doc Holliday replaced Mark Snyder as the Thundering Herd's head football coach in 2010, there was still a lot of leftover buzz around Marshall from the movie, especially around November 14 of each year. Former coaches, players, and administrators, whether they had been involved in the tragedy or not, had been routinely, and were continuing to be interviewed regarding the plane crash for documentaries, news reports, and the like. One day during this time, I was watching television and happened upon an interview with one of these individuals (a former coach, player, or administrator). And there, in the background of this individual's office or a room in his house was an object I never thought I'd see again.

"There's that damn Xavier football!" I exclaimed. "But, what the hell is *he* doing with it?!"

There, the game ball sat as plain as day, decorated with the distinct lettering my daughter had placed on it. I was really pissed. But, I would eventually calm down, recalling a great lesson a wise man once reminded me. It's a practice I've added to my positive way of thinking as I continue to try to repair the damage I've experienced from survivor's guilt: sometimes, it's a good thing to get a second chance. And thus this individual deserved a second chance.

A while back a couple of police officers in the area, including one who was a pretty good friend of mine, encountered somewhat of an unruly crowd in the street. Perhaps seeking to gain the crowd's attention, both policemen fired their guns in the air. Although probably not the smartest or the right thing to do, the gunfire was apparently intended to be nonthreatening and only for attention-getting purposes. Still, the incident caused such a clamor in the area, some community leaders emerged in protest against the policemen, including a member of the '71 Marshall football team who demanded the two officers should be forced to resign. I met with the former player-turned-community leader in defense of the policemen, and argued demanding their resignation was too harsh of a penalty for members of law enforcement who were only trying to gain a disruptive crowd's attention. The former player looked at me, hesitated for a moment, and then shared a story of when he had played football at Marshall.

He told me of a player, also part of the '71 team, who was once caught smoking marijuana by an assistant coach. Although it was the early 1970s and marijuana usage was rampant, Marshall's team rules, per the head coach, stated if you were caught using illegal drugs, you lost your scholarship and were thrown off the team—no questions asked. The coach told the player that he knew the rules, so he might as well pack his bags—he was off the team and out of the program. The player began begging and crying, claiming the assistant didn't have to tell the head coach. "So, in a way, you're asking me to lie to the head coach because you used drugs?!?" the assistant questioned. The player was now sobbing. The assistant coach stared at the player, hesitated for a moment, and then said, "Okay, but no more damn slipups, or then you're definitely gone!" The player agreed and, sure enough, there were no more slipups on his part.

"Do you remember when that happened between you and me, Coach Dawson?" the player asked.

I nodded.

"If you wouldn't have given me a second chance at Marshall and playing football, I tell you one thing, I wouldn't be sitting here today talking to you," he said.

The player in his exact words, and I can still hear it today, added, "Sometimes, it's a good thing to get a second chance."

Representing the group of people, who once wanted the two policemen fired, the '71 player was soon in front of the media, indicating he understood the police had made a stupid mistake, and the community was willing to forgive them—give them a second chance.

Similarly to this football player from the Young Thundering Herd's historic 1971 team, I have fortunately been given a second chance—actually, multiple chances—at Marshall and its football program. If I had not been handed this opportunity, I would not be able to share my story with others. I'd probably be sitting around somewhere still disgruntled with Marshall and certain individuals, having a mind filled with negative thoughts.

I am forever indebted to former Marshall President Stephen Kopp, who suddenly and sadly passed away during this book project in December 2014. Stephen got me out from behind that sycamore tree, and to where I should have been all along—with "my people."

A lot of nice things were said and written about me, like how I "bridged the gap from tragedy to rebirth" of the program in 1971, according to one article. Although honored by such recognition, I was somewhat embarrassed, as well, because I had a great deal of help "bridging" the gap. Assistants Mickey Jackson, Carl Kokor, and Gail Parker went through about as much hell as I did. In recent years, I am glad Mickey, Carl, and I were given the chance to come together again. Although I stayed away for many years, I always loved those men and now cherish each time I'm in their company. After agreeing in 1971 we shouldn't see one another again because of the bad memories the tragedy would likely stir up, Gail and I spoke on the phone a few times, but even those conversations were difficult to get through. I often thank the Old Master for allowing me in 2006 a chance to see and speak with Gail in person for the first time in more than forty years, and for the final time on this earth before he passed away at only sixty-six years old in 2009. Seeing Gail was not nearly as painful as I always imagined it would be, and I will always deeply regret my decision to separate myself.

Because of the movie's publicity, I started to correspond and was placed in the company of some people I had chosen to dodge for a long time, like Jack Lengyel. Honestly, while Jack was head coach with me as an assistant, I was probably jealous of him more than anything else. He was given the opportunity to do what I had started to undertake, and was told I would get a chance to carry out, but never got to: rebuild the Marshall football program. To Jack's credit, because of the mental state I was in at the time, I probably would've had a difficult time working under even Jesus himself if he had been Marshall's head coach. Jack and I eventually had a good conversation and interaction, and were able to hash things out.

But, more so than any of us coaches, the people who deserve the most credit for truly bridging the gap from tragedy to rebirth, in every essence of the expression, were the seventy-five individuals who died in the tragedy and the 1971 Young Thundering Herd players, who were the primary contributors to the rebirth of Marshall football.

Around the time I got reconnected with Gail and Jack, I started to be asked to give speeches. They began at the 2006 Fountain Ceremony, followed by the dedication of the historical marker of the plane crash a few weeks later to—and, I still find this hard to comprehend—eventually different groups all over the country. I found it ironic that people actually wanted me to speak, because I had talked for more than thirty years about everything but the tragedy, but no one listened. So, given the opportunity to talk and finally be heard, I spoke on just about everything, including as much as I could emotionally about the plane crash.

The speech I probably most looked forward to giving was at the Bridgeport Conference Center just outside of Clarksburg, West Virginia, for the Annual Frank Loria Awards Banquet named in honor of my late friend, the College Football Hall of Famer from Virginia Tech. I had been invited to the banquet for years but always declined, always with an excuse. I desperately wanted to come and pay my respects to Frank and his family, but knew I would be asked to speak about certain people or things I simply couldn't talk about. Frank was especially one of them.

I was given another opportunity to attend Frank's banquet, and finally agreed, sometime around 2007, when I thought I wouldn't make an ass of myself by crying and getting emotional. I started off by first thanking the banquet's organizers for giving me another chance to pay tribute to my dear friend. During the speech, I got a little emotional and had to take a couple of "timeouts," but I eventually got through it. I ended my talk by recalling I had heard Virginia Tech head coach Frank Beamer, a teammate of Frank Loria's, asked what he thought would have ever come of Frank if the Marshall plane hadn't crashed. Coach Beamer said it was possible Frank, and not himself, would be the head coach at Virginia Tech, and Beamer his assistant. I added that besides Bobby Bowden and Joe Paterno vying for the most career victories by a Division I head coach, as was the case at the time, it likely would have been a three-man race instead if Frank was still alive.

I don't think I have missed Frank's annual banquet in March ever since attending my first. At the latest one I attended, I had a real senior moment worthy of sharing. There are always several local high-profile football coaches and athletic administrators in attendance at the banquet, and this past year was no different, with then-West Virginia athletic director Oliver Luck present. Like I said, I'll talk about almost everything, so I thought I would take a few friendly and humorous, verbal jabs at Luck. I said how West Virginia wouldn't play Marshall in football when "Oliver Luck" was the Mountaineers quarterback way back when, and with "Oliver Luck" as West Virginia's athletic director the Mountaineers suddenly stopped playing Marshall after seven meetings in a row, and so on. At least three times, I uttered the name "Oliver Luck," or so I thought.

After my speech, this old guy who I chat with every year at the banquet hurried up to me, and closely mumbled so only I could hear, "Red, you don't have shit for sense!"

"I know I don't," I replied confused, "but, what exactly do you mean?"

"Well, you must be watching too much Fox News," he said. "During your whole speech, you kept calling Oliver Luck, 'Oliver North.'"

And, he was correct.

I had mistakenly called Luck "Oliver North" the entire time, so I tried to save a little face: "Well, I know I was calling him that! That was just part of me jabbing at him!"

I hope the Frank Loria Awards Banquet forgives me, and invites me back again next year. Seems like I've asked many people for forgiveness the last decade or so since I started getting my mind right. In the process, I have forgiven a number of people, as well. You see, second chances should work both ways: if you want to receive them, you should also be willing to give them.

About four or five years ago, I contacted the individual who I saw on television with the Xavier game ball in the background. I immediately cut to the chase, making it clear that for one, I was not mad at him. I had spent much of my life staying mad at others, and I was too old to do that any longer. Secondly, I was not going to judge him. There must have been a legitimate reason why a game ball belonging to Marshall was no longer locked in a trophy case but in his possession, so I did not care how he got it. And finally, I informed him that just like he had somehow obtained the ball, he now had a chance—the opportunity—to give it back to Marshall.

He hesitated, stumbled over his words, and then argued the ball I saw on TV was one he had decorated himself to commemorate the win over Xavier in 1971.

"*You* had decorated?" I asked. "Exactly like my daughter decorated mine?"

He didn't respond.

"Look, I don't care how or when, but that football needs to be returned to Marshall," I declared. "And, I'd appreciate it if you would bring it back."

That was the end of our conversation. As I mentioned, that was four or five years ago and, as of the end of the 2014 football season, the ball had yet to be returned. Of course, like me needing multiple chances to associate with the Marshall football program again, this individual may need multiple chances to return the football back to Marshall.

If all the publicity and the increase in the number of enthusiasts for Marshall football ultimately deprived the program of merely a football, we're all in good shape. By talking about the tragedy coupled with trying to avoid negative thoughts, I'm in good shape, dealing with my survivor's guilt better than ever. Fortunately, I have not had a nightmare in a while. With Doc Holliday coaching the Herd, Marshall football is also in good shape—*really* good shape. After winning 10 games in 2013 for the first time in 11 seasons, Marshall won all but one of its 14 games last year.

Although seemingly indecisive, going from being devoted to a university and its football program, to resenting it, only to return to being passionate about it again, I'm now absolutely positive which side of the fence I prefer. Beginning with the university giving me a second chance, Marshall has been very good to me. Whereas I once couldn't fathom entering Fairfield Stadium, I now rarely miss a home game at "The Joan." I especially like the tailgating, and here I didn't even know what the term meant not too terribly long ago. If you're in the area on a game day, come on by. Marshall set me up with a prime tailgating spot, just down from the "We Are Marshall" bronze memorial to the plane crash in the West Lot, directly in front of the main tower. You can't miss me. I'll be the guy everybody is calling "Red" but should be calling "Whitey," and I'll probably have a beer in my hand.

While getting another opportunity to reunite with my Marshall family, I have become closer to my very own family. After my older brother, Jack, died following a long bout with lung cancer, my siblings, Rhett and Lucille, and I were brought a lot closer.

Jack had been in a lot of pain and was very confused. After years of being an airplane pilot for Delta, he routinely believed he was on layover just before he was put into hospice care. That really bothered and got to me. When Rhett and I were together in Canada for his induction into the Saskatchewan Roughriders' Plaza of Honor in 2006, we received the news Jack had died. Several years later, my mother joined him one day before her ninety-seventh birthday.

Although the reality of losing people very close to me is painful, I have been at peace, knowing if they were suffering with pain, like Jack, they no longer have to. And, they all are in a much, much better place.

Whereas I once needed someone to talk to—some counseling—following the plane crash but was too stubborn and naive to seek help, I found myself being a counselor of sorts when those close to us had passed away. A member of my family had a really difficult time dealing with Jack's death. I told her I had learned to first and foremost, get your mind right, away from any constant, tragic thoughts, or you will go through absolute hell. Think positively and talk about your suffering. The more you talk about it, the easier you will be handling it. And, no matter how you feel physically or mentally, get to work—*hard* work. The harder you work, the more your mind is kept occupied.

As for me, when this book is released, I'll soon be turning seventy-three years old. You never know when the Old Master decides it's your turn to go, especially at that age, so I have already made an arrangement or two. I have always thought I would be buried in Valdosta, Georgia. However, in recent years, I have decided when it's time for my spirit to leave this earth, I want my body to join "my people" at Huntington's Spring Hill Cemetery. At the cemetery's highest point overlooking the Marshall campus, I'm planning to reconvene with my old friends, including assistant athletic director Ed Starling, captain of the '71 team, Nate Ruffin, who died in 2001 from leukemia, and the six unidentified bodies from the crash—all players, and all young men I either coached or helped recruit.

Forty-five years later, the tragedy of the plane crash is still like a dream to me. At first, I felt a lot of disbelief and questioned my Heavenly Father. I repeatedly asked myself, "Why would our God, who is all good and loving, allow such a terrible and tragic thing to happen?" I was mad at God. However, in time, I had to get my mind right, determining that the God I worship doesn't interfere with certain things that may cause tragedy. He has a lot of things on his plate to worry about. Still, even with a settled mind, I think it's normal to ask "why": Why did President Kopp pass away so suddenly? Why did my brother undergo such a painful cancer experience? And, why were seventy-five unexpected, innocent people taken on that rainy, foggy night at the Tri-State Airport in 1970?

And, I intend to ask the Old Master "why" when I get "home."